Thinking Careers, Talking Careers

Sarah Lowkis

Thinking Careers, Talking Careers

Published by Lifetime Careers Publishing, 7 Ascot Court, White Horse Business Park, Trowbridge BA14 0XA. www.lifetime-publishing.co.uk

© Lifetime Careers Wiltshire Ltd, 2004

ISBN 1 902876 78 4

Printed and bound by Cromwell Press Ltd, Trowbridge
Cover design by Jane Norman

CONTENTS

About the author

Sarah Lowkis began teaching in secondary comprehensive schools in 1987. Since 1994 she has coordinated careers education and guidance and held responsibility for work experience. In April 2003 she became an Advanced Skills Teacher for careers with county-wide responsibility for improving careers education in schools.

INTRODUCTION

With the introduction of the National Framework for Careers Education 11–19 all schools and sixth-form colleges should make changes to their curriculum. This book is relevant to everyone who teaches careers education in secondary schools and colleges. It provides both practical and theoretical advice for delivering a modern and dynamic careers curriculum. It focuses on four main areas:

- accelerating learning

- inspirational lessons

- lifelong learning

- visionary teacher leadership.

Through exploring learning theories that relate to careers education this book supports teachers in putting in place strategies to empower students to become effective learners. Learning in careers education is about building a structure which facilitates cognitive development. This leads to self-development, and learning will therefore be highly individualised.

As well as educational theory this book provides tried and tested practical ideas. It will enhance teachers' Continued Professional Development (CPD) and lead to greater understanding about teachers as learners. Self-evaluation as a tool for school improvement is stressed throughout the book. Teachers are encouraged to be reflective, critical practitioners who strive for continual improvement and professional competence. For classroom practice to be of a consistently high standard staff must be engaged and motivated. Strong and visionary leadership is essential to facilitate this. In this book we will be exploring strategies for raising the profile of careers education in schools, with an emphasis on ways of raising standards.

Key features of the National Strategy that are succeeding in other curriculum areas are applied to careers education, and good practice in all areas of education is modelled throughout the book.

The following are the core ideas for effective learning in careers.

- The sessions must be fun and engaging.

- Learning outcomes must be sharp, specific and differentiated.

- Different levels of cognitive development will be promoted by use of Bloom's Taxonomy.

- Three-part lessons should be in place, consisting of starter activities, main activities and plenary sessions.

- Relevant learning theories should be understood and applied to accelerate learning within the classroom and beyond.

- Self-evaluation should be integral to the lesson: the teacher and pupils should be able to assess whether the learning outcomes have been met and whether progress has been made.

- Emotional intelligence should be apparent, and used as a tool for empowering pupils.

- An intelligent profiling system should be in place.

- The programme should be coherently linked with citizenship and PSHE.

- There should be high impact on the learner, considering pupils as individuals.

- There must be progression for each individual, not necessarily limited by the key stages.

Chapter 1
EMPOWERING LEARNERS

- Our wonderful brains

- Learners and learning

- Theories of learning relating to careers education

- Key ideas for learning in careers education

- Empowering the learner

- Accelerated learning in careers

- Summary

Our wonderful brains

Our brain is the most complex organ in our body. It weighs around 1.5 kg and is made up of billions of tiny cells called neurones. The neurones are collected together in networks with different regions of the brain being responsible for different jobs. Throughout our lives our brains constantly change, which is called plasticity.

Individual neurones form connections with surrounding neurones in response to change, such as when we are developing as infants, or through damage as a result of an accident, or through learning. As we interact with our surroundings new connections are made and existing connections are strengthened. Connections that are used infrequently become weak or are lost. Learning can be lost if it is not reinforced and used. This can be summed up as **use it or lose it.** An example is learning Spanish at school and not using it again for twenty years until we go on holiday to Spain.

Learning and memory are individual to each person. What each of us remembers about a shared event is different. This is because our brains will have responded differently at the time. Learning is tied to plasticity: new connections are laid down as learning takes place. Whether plasticity occurs or not is linked to the amount of a chemical, glutamate, that is released into the gap between the neurones, known as the synapse. The stronger the impulse, or the higher the frequency of the repetition, the more glutamate is released into the synapse and the stronger the link becomes.

If emotions are triggered at the same time, another chemical is released into the synapse that enhances the effect of the glutamate, and results in stronger connections. This is why we tend to remember happy, sad or painful experiences. It also means that learning is more effective when the emotions are engaged. We also learn better when we pay attention with no distractions, because the release of chemicals into the synapses is centred on one area of the brain. Building on prior experiences, reinforcing and revisiting will strengthen connections and lead to more effective learning.

Thus we learn better if we concentrate, if we link learning to prior experiences, if we are in an emotional state linked to the learning experience, and if we reinforce and revisit. We learn less well if we are distracted, if we do not hang the learning on what has gone before, if we do not go over things, and do not use the new learning. To make the learning meaningful to us we must make sense of it by reusing the learning in a number of different contexts so that a scaffold is constructed around it.

Learners and learning

If you type 'learners and learning' into an internet search engine you will be faced with over 1,500,000 references. It can become a minefield of information which is difficult to navigate successfully. Within this there are at least 50 distinct theories about how people learn. Such a figure may seem off-putting but it need not be so. Every teacher has their own inbuilt value system and appreciation of how children learn. Every day we are presented with success and failure as we unlock learning or hit a brick wall. We use this evidence to construct our own understanding and appreciation of how pupils learn. Once principles of learning are recognised it is beneficial and enlightening to compare our views with other, established ones. Some theories will overlap with our thinking and will help to reinforce beliefs. Other theories will bear no relation to our own working hypotheses and so will be discarded as irrelevant.

Teaching careers education is unlike teaching many other subjects because we are not imparting knowledge and facts to learn. We are promoting an understanding of the world in which we live and encouraging self-development. We are, we hope, equipping pupils with the skills to make value judgements about their futures. The nature of this type of learning is very different to teaching about something concrete. People teaching careers education may have little or no training about how to teach it, and may have little understanding about the type of learning that needs to take place.

As careers education is about self-development, exploration and management (as stated in the three themes of the National Framework for Careers Education) it is vital that the pupil is empowered to take control of their learning. Most of their learning is not going to take place in the classroom but as they encounter everyday situations and interact with others. Teaching in a classroom relies upon pupils being at the same stage of cognitive and emotional intelligence, which of course they are not. Learning is chaotic and cannot be controlled to occur at 9.50 on Tuesday morning because this happens to be the timetabled slot for a careers session.

Our job is to give pupils the skills to make sense of their experiences in a constructive and thought-provoking way, to allow learning to happen and to be recognised. This is why the 'learning outcomes' for a lesson and 'planning for learning' may initially seem contradictory to the notion that learning does not happen in the classroom.

In the classroom we can hope to stimulate thought processes which enable pupils to build up their own value system. This gives them a reference point so that, when a trigger occurs, the brain will make sense of what they are experiencing. Learning will only take place when it is directly relevant and meaningful to them. In this way the brain will make the right connections and store to memory. The more times the memory is retrieved, challenged and reinforced the more effective the learning will be. In a classroom we may stimulate original thoughts, but it is the constant checking and review that will have the most impact.

Theories of learning relating to careers education

As I have said, there are many theories about how children learn, and many can help us to understand how to be effective in teaching careers. The following are some of the theories that support careers education.

Constructivist theory (J. Bruner)

Bruner suggests that learning is an active process whereby learners construct new ideas or concepts based upon their current level of knowledge. The learner selects information, transforms it, constructs hypotheses and makes decisions. The role of the facilitator in learning is to set up the right conditions and to engage the learner in active dialogue.

This theory sits nicely within careers education. Most learning for an individual will happen when they have a need. Our role as teachers of careers is to pose the right question, provide the resources and skills development for pupils to find information, and to have an active dialogue as they process this information. Pupils will select relevant information, ask questions about its validity, pose their own hypothesis about different jobs, training, courses etc, and make decisions. We must make sure that cognitive development is happening so that pupils see beyond the information that is presented.

Bruner states that, in order to learn, pupils must be willing and able to learn. Most learning happens when a person is in a situation where the knowledge and understanding is of immediate use. The curriculum should be spirally organised to allow pupils to revisit and build upon prior understanding. This is reflected in the approach taken by the National Framework for Careers Education: themes reappear throughout the key stages, greater cognitive understanding is sought at each stage, and the suggested activities are based upon everyday experiences. The Framework also encourages pupils to see beyond the information given by challenging their stereotypical view of self.

Social development theory (L. Vygotsky)

Vygotsky's social development theory is based upon the idea that social interaction plays a vital role in the development of cognition. Children's cultural development is based upon interactions with people (interpsychological) and then becomes internalised (intrapsychological). In addition, Vygotsky states that the potential for cognitive development is confined to a time span, 'the zone of proximal development'. Vygotsky also sees learning as being greatly enhanced by social interaction: an individual can learn far more in a collective situation than by themselves. Internalisation can happen after the socially interactive phase.

This theory sits well with the social aspects of self-development. It has been recognised for a long time that pupils benefit greatly from work experience. This learning, which takes place in situ with interaction between the pupil and an instructor, is much deeper than if the same information were taught to a whole class in a school situation. The pupil can constantly build upon their understanding by discussing what they are doing and why. Pupils will often comment, when they have had a good learning experience, that the rest of the staff included them, talked to them and helped them to understand what they were doing.

This may also go some way to explain why some pupils have a bad work experience. Often it occurs when they are isolated physically or socially from the workforce and do not have the opportunity for interaction.

Conditions of learning (R. Gagne)

Gagne identifies five major categories of learning: verbal information, intellectual skills, cognitive strategies, motor skills and attitudes. From these, he recognises a sequence of nine stages to develop true cognitive learning.

- The instructor gains attention: the pupils must connect with the instructor and be receptive to verbal cues.

- The instructor informs the learner of the objectives of their learning, telling them what they are going to learn.

- Recall of prior learning is stimulated by the instructor.

- The instructor presents the stimulus which 'hooks in' the learner.

- The instructor provides learning guidance.

- The instructor elicits performance by the pupil.

- Feedback and reinforcement of learning is provided.

- The pupil and instructor assess and recognise the extent of the learning.

- Knowledge retention is enhanced by transfer to new situations.

These nine stages are the basis of what is recognised to be a model lesson, and all the stages of learning are apparent in a phased lesson. The starter activity engages and links to prior learning; the learning outcomes are sharp and explicit; the teacher teaches a new concept; pupils conduct an activity in a paired or grouped situation based on the new concept; the plenary then encourages feedback and reinforcement with a review of the learning outcomes. Homework is set which enables the learner to reinforce and transform the learning.

Many teachers are using Gagne's theories to structure their lessons, even though they may never have come across his name or read about his theories. The lesson ideas and structures proposed in this book relate to Gagne's 'conditions of learning'. If adopting this approach enhances and accelerates learning in other subjects, it seems logical that structuring careers lessons in this way will have greater impact upon the learner.

Genetic Epistemology (J. Piaget)

Many teachers are familiar with Piaget's work and theories. Most PGCE and BEd courses teach about the cognitive stages he put forward. In his view there are four main stages of a child's cognitive development, known as the Schemas. They are age-dependent and sequential, and children will only be receptive to learning if it is based upon their current cognitive stage of development. The four stages are:

- sensorimotor (0-2 years), where intelligence takes the form of motor actions

- pre-operation (3-7 years), where intelligence is intuitive

- concrete operations (8-11 years), where intelligence is logical but based upon concrete examples and references

- formal operations (12-15 years), where intelligence is based upon abstract ideas.

Piaget proposes that each stage of intelligence has many aspects of learning within it and this learning must take place before the next stage of intelligence can be accessed. Although the stages are age-dependent, different children will reach them at different ages.

These ideas offer principles that apply to all aspects of teaching and can be applied to careers teaching.

- Children will give different explanations of reality based upon their stage of development.

- Cognitive development involves engagement and adaptation.

- Activities must be based at the appropriate level of cognitive development to allow pupils to engage in learning.

- Teaching methods must actively involve pupils and present them with challenge.

These theories will have a bearing upon careers teaching. There is now a statutory duty to provide careers education in years 7 and 8. According to Piaget, pupils in these year groups will be at different stages of cognitive development. Some pupils will be at the concrete operational stage and will need examples from within their own direct experience so that they can relate to them. Other pupils in the same class will be at the formal operational stage and will need to be presented with challenges that involve abstract thought.

The progression of themes through the framework should build upon these stages. In year 11 there will still be some pupils at the concrete stage who will need a different curriculum to other pupils.

For example, in using careers software pupils at the concrete stage will learn best from using a visual and factual programme such as CID (careers information database) whereas other pupils would find this boring and need a programme which involves abstract thought such as Fast Tomato. For pupils' research during work experience, it may be relevant for those at the concrete stage to find out facts about the company where they are placed. Pupils at the formal stage may be asked to make observations about how people interact, and to identify which aspects of communication lead to people working together effectively.

Conversation theory (G. Pask)

Pask has based his theory upon the idea that learning occurs through conversations about subject matter by which knowledge is made explicit. He states that conversations can occur on three levels: natural language (general discussion), object language (discussing subject matter) and metalanguage (discussing learning). To Pask the critical teaching method is to 'teachback' what has been learned to a peer. This makes the knowledge explicit and involves manipulation which develops understanding. These aspects of Pask's theory sit comfortably with the idea of constructive learning. Careers education lends itself to this because there are ample opportunities for pupils to feed back what they have learned to teachers and to peers.

The theories of Bruner, Vygotsky, Gagne, Piaget and Pask are a small sample of the numerous theories about how learning occurs. Other theories will also show parallels with learning theories in careers.

Key ideas for learning in careers education

From these theories key ideas can be taken and used to accelerate learning in careers education, all of them putting the learner at the centre, with teachers as guides and facilitators. Among the chief key ideas for learning in careers education are the following.

- **Connecting with pupils:** in all effective teaching the teacher must exude an energy which connects with pupils and makes them receptive to learning. This is not easily quantifiable and everybody has the ability to engage to differing degrees. Nevertheless, in careers teaching it is vital because pupils' learning is dependent on what they take with them out of the classroom and into a situation where deep learning can take place. For example, in an assembly preparing a year group for work experience I explained about the need to have a 'go-for-it winning attitude'. The following week I visited a boy on work experience at a garage. At school he had been disengaged. In the workplace he was the best pupil that the garage owner had ever had. He was enthusiastic, one step ahead in anticipating the mechanic's next move, always ready with the correct tool and asking questions, eager to learn. I asked the boy why he was different in the workplace. He said that he had listened in assembly and had come determined to do his best and put himself forwards rather than shrinking back. In this example something said in assembly must have connected with the boy. He changed his usual mode of behaviour and attitude and was basking in the rewards of doing so. Unfortunately connectivity is difficult to plan for. With any group of people you will connect with some and not with others.

- **Structuring lessons:** Gagne's sequence of nine stages of cognitive development can be used to structure lessons. This should be considered when putting together schemes of work and lesson plans and will help to accelerate the learning.

- **Autonomous learning:** learning must be autonomous, i.e. pupils will become self-governing and be able to work under their own direction. This is vital for careers education because so much of it is personal to an individual, and the learning will take place out of the classroom and not during a guided lesson. For example, a pupil will recognise when they need to make a decision between two possible career pathways. They will use the skills that they have been taught to research the options and use tools for decision making that have been modelled to them. The teacher has provided the necessary skills and knowledge for the pupil to become autonomous.

- **Active learning:** learning must be active, not passive. The teacher's role is not to impart knowledge but to develop deep understanding. To achieve active learning a pupil must be fully engaged mentally. Active learning involves decision making, talking, explaining ideas, listening to ideas and giving responses, performing, planning, reviewing and prioritising. Thus if, when pupils are to use a website to research a job, the teacher tells a pupil which website to use and lists questions that need answers, then the pupil is learning passively. If a pupil has to decide which of two websites to use and which information to select for a particular purpose, then the process becomes active.

- **Constructive learning:** constructivism leads to insightful learning rather than surface learning. With constructivism the learner constructs knowledge from resources. The teacher's role is to provide the resources and the stimulus to allow the learner the opportunity to learn and to look for meaning behind facts. During the discovery process the learner should be engaged in dialogue about their thought processes. Thus a teacher leading a lesson on recognising bias in information would provide suitable resources such as college prospectuses, careers information leaflets, such as CLIPS leaflets from Lifetime Careers Publishing, *Working in . . .* books, magazines, websites and publicity brochures from companies and professional organisations. If a constructive approach is applied, the teacher may pose the question, 'What do you think bias is? Tell me by the end of the session.' Pupils are given the opportunity to develop their own views and understanding by constructing knowledge. The teacher is a learning facilitator.

Summary of key ideas

These ideas are not mutually exclusive and they all have their place in a three-part or phased lesson. The principles of autonomy, active learning and constructivism can be used throughout the careers curriculum. Putting them in the context of a lesson ensures that pupils understand not only **what** they are learning but, just as importantly, **how** they are learning. The ultimate goal is that pupils should have the skills and understanding to construct their own knowledge, to gain insight into this knowledge, and to find meaning. This will enable them to make effective decisions about the way they lead their life now and in the future.

Empowering the learner

Once the teacher has developed their own value base about how pupils learn, it becomes easier to enter the mindset of not what to teach but how to teach it in the most effective way. The first stage is to identify which concepts and principles you are hoping the pupil will learn. Then from these you need to develop sharp learning outcomes, which are differentiated and can be shared by the teacher and learner.

The next stage is to follow Gagne's list for the sequence of a lesson and use it as a check list. How will attention be gained? How will the teacher connect and identify with the pupils? How will the learning outcomes be linked to prior learning and recall? What will be the stimulus to engage the learner? Think of a high impact, fun starter activity which actively involves the whole class. How will you teach the main concepts or principles? How will all pupils participate in an activity which will be challenging to them, involve 'teachback' and collaborative working? How will their findings be shared and reinforced? How will the learning outcomes be reviewed? What opportunities can you give the pupils to transfer their learning to a new situation?

Besides these questions proposed by Gagne there are further questions to address if you are taking the constructivist approach to preparing your lesson.

- What learning is expected?

- How can you allow pupils to construct their own knowledge and arrive at their own reality?

- How will you prompt pupils to guide them through an activity instead of issuing a sequence of instructions to the whole class?

- What opportunities will there be for pupils to make decisions?

- How will you interact with individuals to elicit a learning response?

- How can you ensure that the learning will continue beyond the classroom?

If you are asking yourself these questions and planning lessons accordingly then you are working towards empowered learners.

Pupils must be developing the confidence and skills to be autonomous to allow them to grow and carry out the research that is needed at each stage of self-development. Pupils need to be made aware of how the learning outcomes of lessons should be transferred to their individual research and outcomes. Follow-up activities must be clearly stated to prompt and guide pupils so that they know to access a learning opportunity. Not all pupils will be ready at the same stage and so a spiralling approach is needed where ideas are revisited. Careers guidance interviews provide a powerful opportunity for guiding an individual towards the level of learning that is appropriate to their needs.

Accelerated learning in careers

Accelerated learning will happen when the learning theories are translated into practice and have impact in the classroom. Here are the top ten principles for putting accelerated learning into practice. They are central to effective teaching and learning and should apply to careers as well as all other subjects.

- Plan each lesson for learning and base activities around this, instead of planning the activities first.

- Transform the learning objectives into sharp learning outcomes that are differentiated and include numerical targets.

- Make the learning outcomes explicit at the start of the lesson and refer to them throughout the lesson so that the purpose is always kept in focus.

- Have a starter activity which is engaging and sets the foundation for the learning that is to take place.

- Build upon prior knowledge.

- Plan lessons which are varied and make sure the learning activities can be accessed by pupils with different learning styles.

- Empower the learner by applying learning theories.

- Encourage emotional awareness.

- Use self-evaluative strategies during a lesson to assess whether learning has taken place.

- Use plenary sessions to reinforce the learning and to link to further opportunities for self-development.

Summary

Teaching careers is often different to teaching other subject areas because there is no distinct body of knowledge to be delivered. The learner needs to be empowered to use the skills and awareness to carry on learning out of a classroom situation. Learning theories can be applied which enable this to happen. The pupils should experience accelerated learning in the classroom to maximise the effect of learning beyond the classroom. The lesson experience should be the structure upon which the pupil can build their self-development.

Chapter 2
IMPROVING CAREERS

- The importance to pupils of effective careers education

- The importance to schools of effective careers education

- The status of careers education in schools

- How to raise the status

- How to improve the delivery

- How to improve the impact

- Summary

The importance to pupils of effective careers education

One of the theories of guidance is that by the age of three children have conceived an idea about what they want to do when they grow up. This conception is based upon their direct experience of the world around them. There will be people who influence their lives whom they set as role models. Also, by the age of three a child will have formed ideas about women's and men's jobs. These ideas are not based upon knowledge of the options available to them, but upon where they see themselves in the society in which they live. It is also a fact that most, but not all, children stay in their self-created stereotypical role and that this is continually reinforced by those around them. How often, as teachers, do we hear boys asking to go into building trades and then, when we probe further, find that Dad or an uncle is a builder? Teachers breed teachers, hairdressers breed hairdressers, doctors follow family lines and so on.

If this is so, then we owe it to children to give them alternatives upon which to base their decisions. Self-esteem must be built up to a point where self-belief is strong enough to realise ambitions. We must allow the development of skills to overcome barriers. It takes a strong and self-assured individual to break out of the family mould and social constraints into which they are born.

I recently taught a boy in the sixth form who was doing A levels in geography, biology and English. I took him away on a field trip to study plant succession on a sand dune. On the second morning of the field trip, as he stood on the top of a ridge looking out to sea across a deserted beach, he started yelling at the top of his voice and then ran down the sand dune. When I got to him he was sitting quietly crying, unusual for a six foot three seventeen year old. I asked him what the matter was, but he couldn't tell me. Later in the evening we sat and talked. He told me that when he was only five his Dad had died, leaving money in trust for him to go to university. This was unusual because nobody in recent family history had gone to university, or even stayed at school for further study. He told me that during years 10 and 11 he was predicted Ds and Es for his GCSEs, as were all his group of friends. At night they would hang around the streets drinking and getting up to trouble with people who had already left school a couple of years earlier. One day he woke up having dreamed about his Dad. He had a tremendous sense of guilt that he was failing to fulfil his Dad's ambitions for him. He saw his future mapped out ahead of him, hanging around the streets. He decided to change and to go it alone, rather than follow his friends. He identified with some teachers who had faith in his abilities and worked closely with them to bring up his grades. As a result he got into the sixth form to take A levels.

So why was he crying on a sand dune? Up to that point he had not known what he wanted to do. But, looking at the sand dunes and plants, he suddenly realised that he was enjoying what he was doing and that he wanted to follow this as a career. It was as if his Dad was standing proudly next to him, and he experienced complete joy and sadness all at once. Later on that year he went to university to study environmental geography.

Here is an example of a boy who could have followed a stereotypical pathway but had the strength of character to sacrifice friendships and childhood bonds to realise an ambition. He had the support of teachers who told him he could do it, and he had the driving force of wanting to please his dead father.

There are some key things here. This boy had people who gave him the attention, support and care he needed; and he was working to seek the approval of an influential figure in his life (albeit sadly a departed one). He also had guidance and knew what goal he needed to aim for to realise his ambition.

Our job in careers education is to give all pupils the best possible life chances. At the very least we want to prevent young people from dropping off the bottom and out of society. Pupils therefore need to gain the best qualifications they can and find opportunities to develop skills, qualities and self-belief. We need to be instrumental in guiding pupils through transitions and decision points, and challenge the stereotypical roles that have been set for them. If pupils are going to aim high they need to be self-aware and be presented with all the possible pathways open to them, not just the ones with which they are familiar through upbringing.

Effective careers education is vital to give pupils the knowledge and skills upon which they can make informed decisions about their future. If we are simply reinforcing stereotypes then pupils very early become pigeonholed and run the risk of not fulfilling their true potential. Poor careers education leads to pupils without clear goals and aspirations who drift through their school time in an aimless and unguided way, with nothing to work towards. This leads to poor motivation and lack of success.

The importance to schools of effective careers education

The importance of effective careers education to a school is directly linked to the benefits to pupils. If pupils are set clear goals and are motivated to do well, their attainment will go up. Not only will the outcomes be higher in terms of GCSE grades but pupils will buy into school and contribute to the wider school community. Children are more likely to become active citizens behaving responsibly towards each other if their projected image of themselves is one of success in society. This means that pupils are more engaged in lessons and are prepared to take responsibility for their own learning. All this leads to much better working conditions for teachers.

Sadly, many senior managers are slow to see the link. Often careers coordinators are given little time or support to carry out anything more than general maintenance tasks in their role. Their time and energy can easily be used up with administration and talking to pupils, at the expense of improving the careers curriculum and guidance procedures which would benefit all pupils. All schools aim to improve standards, but many have yet to recognise the importance and huge potential of developmental work in careers in achieving this aim.

The status of careers education in schools

Careers education often suffers from low status in schools. There are several reasons for this.

- Although careers education is statutory, the Framework for its delivery is only recommended, not mandatory. The Framework was made non-statutory to allow schools flexibility in delivering the curriculum in creative ways, relevant to their own pupils' needs. However, some schools have taken this to mean that large parts of the Framework can be ignored completely, and other sections reduced to a bare minimum. Compared to citizenship, which is statutory, careers is often seen as of less importance.

- Schools have no legal requirement for reporting on careers, whereas they do for citizenship.

- Careers is not examined and so can be seen as unworthy of specified delivery time.

- There is no training or qualifications for careers teaching before a teacher takes on the role.

- There is only one careers coordinator in a school, so few people recognise the diverse nature of the role.

- In many schools there is no recognisable careers team, so it becomes difficult to have a forum in which to spread the word and to implement developmental changes.

- Careers coordinators are often left out of meeting structures and left off circulation lists.

- Careers developmental work is often not fed into the school development plan.

- Nobody trains to be a careers teacher. The role is therefore always seen as secondary to the main teaching subject and is often tagged onto the role of a tutor, which is itself wrongly seen as a low priority for teachers.

This list does not make comfortable reading: no specialist staff, no curriculum time, non-statutory framework, etc.

However, our job is to raise the status of careers education and to drive change forward to improve the experiences of young people. There are many good and high profile features of careers education which give hope that we can influence others and bring about effective change. Among the positive factors are the following.

- Many people will be involved in teaching careers. Provided you have the opportunity to work directly with them, you can influence the way in which they work.

- You can model good practice in meetings where you have input, in lesson plans and in the quality of learning experiences that you provide for the pupils. Your influence will affect all young learners in a school.

- You are providing support for many staff in key roles around the school. You will be working directly with both middle managers and senior managers.

- You are the only expert in the school in this field, so you provide vision and voice at a whole-school level.

- Careers is seen as important and relevant to pupils. It directly affects all of their lives and has meaning and consequence for them, unlike some subject areas that are abstract and removed from their everyday experiences.

- Many staff will enjoy teaching careers, as opposed to other aspects of PSHE, because they can identify with it and see its relevance for young people.

- You are seen by pupils as somebody who can help them and so you will often have very positive relationships with challenging pupils.

- You have links with outside agencies and employers who can support you in developing and delivering the curriculum.

How to raise the status

The status of careers education within a school is influenced by both positive and negative factors. To enhance the status of careers education in your school you need to maximise the positive factors so that the negative factors no longer prevent progress.

The first priority is to cultivate a vision for careers. Once you are clear about why you are doing careers education and what you want to achieve, you will be able to communicate your values effectively whilst maintaining your integrity. Ensure that your vision fits in with that of the school, as this will support your cause. You will also need a supportive voice amongst the senior management team: this may be your line manager or it may be another ally with whom you work closely and effectively. It is worth fostering this support so that any proposals that are discussed at whole-school level are more likely to gain support. Make sure that you have an input into the school development or improvement plan. Follow the planning cycle and make sure that you link with heads of year and heads of faculty when your developments are being implemented through their teams. This then means that you have joint investment in making these developments successful.

Secondly, make sure you are reliable, effective and punctual in delivering your materials. You will need to produce lesson plans and resources in time for heads of year to disseminate the information to their team, if this is the way your school operates. Make sure that you have a sequence of lessons done in advance that forms a coherent package and makes the learning explicit. Spend time modelling high-impact activities for colleagues in a way which will engage them. In this way, they are more likely to feel confident when delivering the activities to pupils and more likely to focus on the learning if it is made explicit. Similarly, if you are responsible for a sequence of lessons then launch it with something fun and hard hitting.

Thirdly, try to lead by example and have pride in what you do. Colleagues will trust you if you are consistent in your values and put into practice what you preach. If you give mixed messages people will discount what you have to say, making it difficult to bring about change within your institution: your ideas will seem to be based upon thin air rather than firm ground. What you say must have high currency if you are going to influence other people in the way they work. It is about building up professional trust. If you prove trustworthy with a wide range of different people then word will get around the school that you are someone whose opinions are valid. Teachers are very quick to point out shortcomings in each other and to undermine one another. We often look for the Achilles heel without recognising all the positive things about the way in which someone works.

Fourthly, publicise your successes – but subtly! Don't boast or exaggerate about how wonderfully the pupils are doing every week. But evaluate what you do and publish your findings to senior managers. Celebrate success in newsletters, using pupil quotes where you can and cultivating your own newshound team. Take photos and have sound bites with them for display around the school. Do not shy away from public forums such as information evenings for parents: they present good opportunities to be on show.

How to improve the delivery

As we have said, most teachers will not be passionate about delivering careers education and may regard it as a low priority. It is a real bonus to find a colleague who is sympathetic and willing to work with you; you are far more likely to be creative and inventive with someone else to bounce ideas off. Otherwise, you simply have to make things as straightforward and easy for colleagues as you can. Do this by:

- having clear sharp learning outcomes that are stated on the lesson plan

- having a three-part lesson plan with a starter activity that engages the pupils

- making the lessons fun, using a wide variety of learning styles

- modelling lessons by team teaching, videoing activities to show in training sessions, or by getting teachers to do a shortened version of the activities

- giving lesson plans and resources together and in advance, with clearly defined times when support will be given

- showing the progression and coherence within sequences of lessons

- evaluating success as you go along, which will encourage a professional dialogue about what works well.

Staff are put off by careers activities if they cannot grasp what learning is taking place, if the materials are shabby and outdated, or if they are given no support about strategies for delivering the subject. A teacher given photocopied sheets at the last minute with little or no explanation can hardly be expected to form a high view of careers education. If you are rigorous, consistent and supportive you will find that teachers are pleased to teach careers because it is something tangible and relevant for everyone.

It is important also to monitor what is being delivered. This is easiest if you can drop into the teaching bases during the session, either informally or for a formal evaluation through a lesson observation. If you are not available, then a head of year may be in the position to do this for you. This will help to establish which staff are delivering the curriculum and which are doing their own thing. Your findings may lead to difficult conversations with members of staff, but this is not your direct responsibility. If a member of staff is failing to deliver the curriculum, you should offer support, monitor the situation over a period of time, then, if necessary, gather the evidence and refer upwards. In the best case the support offered at the monitoring stage will rectify the problem before it becomes a major issue.

How to improve the impact

If all the other strategies are put into place then the impact upon the learner should be high. For success you need:

- a well planned curriculum

- a good set of lesson plans

- pace, variety and challenges in activities

- motivated and confident teachers delivering the lessons

- high profile for careers on a school level.

All this will take time to develop and build up. You will probably need a three-year development process before you can establish whether you have made a real difference. Much of the evidence for impact will be anecdotal, so it is important to look at evidence from self-evaluation to get a more accurate picture.

Summary

Careers education may be used as a tool for improvement in a school. This is done by motivating pupils to do well through raising aspirations and giving clear goals. This must be supported by an effective careers programme that is delivered well throughout the school. This is more likely to happen if careers has a high status in the school and senior management recognise its importance.

Chapter 3
SELF-EVALUATION

- What is self-evaluation?
- Introducing self-evaluation to a team
- Strategies for pupil self-evaluation
- Strategies for teacher self-evaluation
- Improving teaching and learning
- Summary

What is self-evaluation?

Self-evaluation is a process in which an organisation or an individual, through systems and procedures at the heart of their day-to-day practice, is able to reflect upon what they do. A self-evaluative organisation or individual is always striving to refine, improve and transform. A self-evaluative organisation or individual does not need to be inspected by an outside body or person to know how well they are doing. The assessment comes from within.

Self-evaluation is central to careers education. True self-evaluation leads to improvement in pupils' achievements and opportunities. If your school is not yet operating within a self-evaluative framework you are in a prime position to be a leader in this field of development. If your school has gone some way towards having a framework in place, you will be able to try out some ideas and feed back to departments. Careers education can become the exemplar of good practice which models effective teaching and learning across all subject areas.

Self-evaluation exists on four levels:

- whole school
- careers team
- teachers
- pupils.

To be effective, self-evaluation must start within the classroom and be part of daily practice and classroom management. There must be self-evaluation by the pupils which enables them to take responsibility for their own learning. There must also be self-evaluation by the classroom teachers so that they take on responsibility for the learning that is to take place in their classroom. It is not acceptable to blame schemes of work, resources or the behaviour of children. With self-evaluation come the skills to unpick exactly what has taken place, with solutions for making it better next time, both with the group and the topic area covered. The purpose is to act upon the information received to make teaching and learning more effective in every classroom. The best teachers are reflective practitioners who continually learn and refine what they do.

Self-evaluation can leave both the pupil and the teacher feeling raw and vulnerable if it is mishandled. It is only effective within an atmosphere of mutual trust and respect. Both parties must be sufficiently emotionally aware that findings are not taken as personal criticisms but as ways of moving forward. The climate needs to be right within the classroom and within the organisation for people to be open and responsive to findings. As well as informing practice within the classroom, there will be issues arising from self-evaluation that are pertinent to the whole team, relating to both classroom management and curriculum delivery. In addition there may be issues that are relevant to the whole school.

From effective self-evaluation comes effective change. When individuals work collaboratively there is collective knowledge and commitment. This fosters an atmosphere where professional learning is at its strongest. It directly identifies the issues that an organisation faces and solutions are therefore directly relevant. This is different to applying models that have been devised externally, which are not fit for their purpose.

Introducing self-evaluation to a team

One way to introduce self-evaluation to your team is to carry out an audit. This helps to raise awareness, but it also reassures colleagues that they are already doing much that is required: sometimes all that is needed is to look at existing good practice in a different way.

Opposite is an example of an audit, which can be modified to suit your own institution. It can be done with individuals in a team or across a whole school by each team. An audit such as this is a good way of finding a base line and for judging individuals' perceptions.

Audit of self-evaluation

Importance attached		How well this reflects your school
Low High 1 2 3 4 5		Low High 1 2 3 4 5
	We create a positive learning environment where different learning styles are valued.	
	We share learning outcomes with pupils.	
	Opportunities are given within each lesson for pupils to reflect on what they have learnt.	
	We encourage pupils to assess their own work.	
	We see making mistakes as a way of improving.	
	We openly talk about our shortcomings and seek ways of improving.	
	Teachers incorporate targets in their discussions with pupils.	
	We share achievements with pupils. Teachers give formative feedback that supports and motivates pupils.	
	Modelling is seen as an effective approach to encouraging self-evaluation.	
	Pupils' feedback is given to staff and changes are made as a result.	
	Oral work is seen as a method of assessing learning.	
	Pupils are encouraged to describe the process of learning.	

Following this a yearly plan should be put into place to coordinate the evaluation and to ensure that it is progressive. Findings should be reported and discussed at predetermined review points. A yearly cycle of self-evaluation may look something like this:

	Sept	Oct	Nov	Dec	Jan	Feb	Mar	Apr	May	Jun	Jul
Peer observation		▓	▓								
Team leader observation							▓	▓			
Work sampling					▓						
Pupil interviews									▓		
Pupil questionnaire						▓					
Evaluation meeting				▓		▓		▓		▓	

Ideally this would fit into a whole-school strategy on self-evaluation. If not, then produce one for careers and let the senior management team know about it as a way towards self-improvement. By careers having its own self-evaluation calendar the status of careers education is raised.

Strategies for pupil self-evaluation

Strategies should start within the classroom and radiate outwards. Areas to consider are:

- plenaries

- peer assessment

- question and answer activities

- pupil questionnaires

- pupil focus groups

- work sampling

- data analysis

- classroom observation

- evaluative meetings.

Plenaries

Pupil self-evaluation is vital to maximise learning capacity. Setting sharp learning outcomes allows pupils to judge whether they have been successful in their learning. This should be integral to all lessons, including careers lessons and activities such as work experience.

The general principle is that there must be review points in the lesson. In the simplest case, there would be a collective review of the learning outcomes at the end of the lesson. A quick and effective tool is the Thumb Response: thumbs up, thumbs sideways, thumbs down. The pupils gather around the board where the learning outcomes are displayed. The teacher reads out each outcome and asks each pupil to give a thumb response:

- thumbs up – I really get it

- thumbs sideways – still a bit unsure

- thumbs down – I didn't get it at all.

This is great when used with the 'all, most, some' model of learning outcomes. The teacher can judge their own expectations of students as well as engaging students in reviewing their learning. You may well find that there is a shift in expectation with the majority of the pupils being able to answer positively to the 'some' outcome. This is because when the learning is explicit, pupils naturally aim high.

There are many variations on this theme. Pupils can use red, amber and green flash cards to indicate learning, or they can give themselves a score.

Peer assessment

Peer assessment, if done correctly, is a powerful self-evaluative tool. This model is reflective, and helps towards closing the learning gap between high- and low-attaining pupils. It is useful for producing good quality extended writing. Peer assessment can involve producing CVs, writing personal statements about work experience, and producing an 'all about me' top sheet for progress files.

The key steps to peer assessment are as follows.

- A learning outcome is set and shared with the class.

- Thought shower is used to establish success criteria: how will you know if you have achieved it?

- Pupils are encouraged to set their own success criteria.

- During an activity pupils are stopped and asked to read through and check their own work.

- Pupils swap with a partner and read through each other's work.

- Pupils are asked to identify something good in their partner's work.

- Without being reminded of the success criteria, pupils' comments tend to be general or hinge on presentation.

- After another period of work repeat the process, this time reminding pupils of the success criteria and learning outcome. All comments must now be related to these.

- The pair together agree on how the work could be improved, and further work time is allowed for these improvements to be carried out.

Pupil self-assessment has many benefits.

- Pupils understand what they are learning.

- They are more motivated during an activity.

- They agree what is a successful outcome.

- Self-esteem is developed.

- Independent self-improvement skills are taught.

- The quality of work improves.

- The learning becomes more focused.

Strategies for teacher self-evaluation

Question and answer activities

The main concept here is that the teacher knows precisely what learning they want to take place and he or she uses tools to check understanding during the lesson. During activities the teacher must be circulating and engaging pupils, either individually or as a whole class, in meaningful conversations based around the learning outcomes. Questioning must be effective to elicit understanding.

Unproductive questions include 'How are you getting on then?' 'On to question five yet? Well, why not?' 'Why haven't you got a pen?' These do not inform the teacher about the pupil's understanding, nor do they engage the pupil in productive thought. Set pupils a goal. For example, during a lesson placing job roles in chronological order, give the pupils guidance by saying, 'When I come round to you, I want you to give me three changes in work pattern that you have noticed.' This puts an edge onto the lesson from the beginning and increases the challenge. It gives a good opportunity to 'catch pupils being good', to offer instant praise and reward for being on task and solving the problem. The purpose is to assess the level of understanding. If a pupil cannot spot one pattern, then a different approach and 'catch up' may be needed, e.g. another pupil could be asked to explain the thought processes they went through to arrive at their conclusions, so modelling the thought processes.

Whole class questioning can be very effective but it can also be very weak. It should be used to engage thought and present challenge. That means that all pupils must be involved. In poor examples pupils are allowed to put their hands up to contribute. This usually results in confident boys being allowed to dominate, with others switching off, knowing that they are 'off the hook'. For many years, the use of open questions has been suggested as the key to effective questioning. The more recent rule is that it takes pupils approximately seven seconds to think, so time must be allowed between the question being posed and the response being given. A simple way of ensuring this is to operate a 'hands down policy'. The teacher is then in control and can direct the questions at specific individuals. This means that the more demanding questions based on the more challenging learning outcomes can be directed at the most able pupils. Likewise, questions based upon the lower-level learning outcomes can be addressed at the less able pupils. Ask the question, allow seven seconds' thinking time and then name the individual. Explain the seven-second rule: all must be thinking of an answer; and the time does NOT begin after the name is called; a response is expected immediately.

At the start of the lesson questioning sets the pace, context and thought patterns. It can help establish prior understanding. During and at the end of the lesson it becomes a self-evaluative tool to check the learning that has taken place.

Another method that works well is the bouncing ball technique. Pupils stand in a circle and bounce a ball to each other. When a pupil catches the ball they have to shout out an answer to a question such as, 'Give skills that are important during work experience' or 'Name jobs that involve working outdoors'.

Individual wipe boards are very versatile and a must in every classroom. Place T on one side and F on the other to indicate responses to true or false questions, or individual responses to understanding checks related to the learning outcomes. Both the pupil and the teacher can then see whether the expected learning has taken place.

Pupil questionnaires

Pupil satisfaction questionnaires work well. Prepare a series of questions which pupils answer by circling a number on a four-point scale. Using a four-point scale prevents pupils 'opting out' by choosing a midpoint. Here is an example used for students at the end of year 9 with their tutors.

How satisfied are you with your careers lessons? *(Please make sure that you put your own ideas down.)*

For each of the following questions below circle a score of 1 to 4, where:

    1 = Yes, definitely.   3 = No, not really.
    2 = Yes, to a certain extent.   4 = No, definitely not.

Do you feel that you have made good progress in careers lessons this year?	1	2	3	4
Do you know what you have to do in careers' lessons to improve?	1	2	3	4
Are you receiving the support from your teacher that you need to make good progress?	1	2	3	4
Are the expectations of the teacher high?	1	2	3	4
Do you come to lessons prepared to learn?	1	2	3	4
Is the discipline within the class good?	1	2	3	4
Are you clear about what you are expected to learn each lesson?	1	2	3	4
Does the teacher explain things in a clear way?	1	2	3	4
Were you aware of the options that were available to you?	1	2	3	4
Did you receive enough support and guidance in making your choices?	1	2	3	4
Do you feel that you have been helped to make informed choices and career plans?	1	2	3	4

What would help you to learn more effectively?

Do you need any additional support and guidance?

A questionnaire such as the above can be adapted and used at any point in the course. It can also be used across a series of classes or tutor groups to check consistency by team leaders. Pupils respond well if they are given the opportunity to see the class findings and to discuss the outcomes. If done well the findings can be used as a lever to bring about change within the classroom. There may be simple things, such as rearranging the seating, that can be easily done but have a big impact on the group. When I did this with my tutor group many of them commented on three loud boys who dominated the group by always positioning themselves in my eye line during discussions whilst others felt marginalised. The class decided that a way forward would be to have these particular boys sitting at the edge of the group. Without being asked, on the next occasion they did this and no longer dominated. This raised my awareness of the classroom dynamics as well as allowing the pupils to take on responsibility for their learning.

Pupil focus groups

Structured pupil interviews can be used for self-evaluation and produce a great deal of information. This method can be used with teaching groups, tutor groups or after big events such as work experience. Choose pupils carefully. They must be willing to discuss things openly and not be under peer pressure. A cross section of three to four without any friendship groups is usually successful. Prepare the questions in advance. A general chat may or may not throw up useful information so think about the specific outcomes that you want. Choose when and where you meet: it is often more effective to have neutral ground. Make the ground rules and the purpose clear: you want to find out their opinions on a range of issues to allow you and the class to work more effectively together. It is not an appreciation society nor is it a battle field. You may wish to tape-record or video the discussion. If you do this you can use it for coaching other staff in the technique, and it then becomes useful for consistency in team approach.

There are a wide variety of useful questions to pose.

- Give three things that are good about careers lessons.

- Give three things that are not good about careers lessons.

- In which lesson did you learn the most?

- What was it about the lesson that helped you to learn?

- In which lesson did you not learn effectively?

- What was it about this lesson that meant you did not learn?

- If you had to use three words to describe me as a teacher what would they be?

- How could the lessons be improved?

- Do you think that you are making good progress in careers lessons?

- How do you know?

- Do you know what you have to do to improve?

This takes a very personal approach and will only work with pupils who will be honest. Depending upon your situation better results may be obtained by swapping teachers so that it is one step removed. This technique can be used by team leaders to monitor the effectiveness of teaching across a year group. Think through carefully what you will do with the information. It can lead to tricky conversations if a can of worms is opened, but sometimes this needs to be done to raise standards.

Work sampling

Work sampling is a technique used by team leaders, in this instance careers coordinators or heads of year. A topic is chosen by the team leader, e.g. progress files, and a date is set, usually at a team meeting, for all the team to bring along three examples from their group across the ability range. Work sampling has several benefits. It is a way of sharing good practice between the teachers, as everyone will have a different approach and different outcomes. It flags up the importance of consistency in ensuring that all teachers are delivering what they say they are. It is also a way of looking across a team at shared strengths and shared weaknesses. Listing team strengths is morale-boosting and if there are weaknesses then collective problem solving will lead to the best solutions.

Data analysis

Data analysis is difficult in careers education because the content is not assigned levels nor is it examined. Effective careers education and guidance leads to improved attainment across all subjects, but such improvement is, of course, dependent upon so many variables that it would be hard to argue that an increase in pupils attaining five A*-Cs at GCSE was down to improved careers and guidance. It is true that, in schools that have effective careers and guidance, value-added scores are generally high, but this is probably due to the teaching ethos of the whole organisation.

More quantifiable data to inform your practice can be generated from pupil and employer feedback forms. Below is an example of data generation used to evaluate work experience with pupils. Again the four-point scale is used so that pupils have to make a decision, and cannot opt for a mid-point. The percentages show the information that is generated. If you want to compare tutor groups or look at gender differences then sort the forms before collation. The processing is time-consuming and union guidance would state that this should not be a teacher's role. Make sure you have administration time allocated or ask reliable pupil volunteers.

The questions are placed chronologically, starting with the preparation for the placement and leading on to the placement itself. Pupils' names were not put on the questionnaires but the name of the placement was. This allows monitoring of individual placements as well as the in-school procedures.

Work experience evaluation 2003

Results from 144 returns expressed as %.

A = Yes, definitely   B = Yes, to a certain extent   C = No, not really   D = No, definitely not

		A	B	C	D
1	It was made clear to me why I was doing work experience.	54	39	7	0
2	I knew how to arrange my placement.	59	40	1	0
3	I was given enough support to make sure that I got the right placement for me.	40	56	2	2
4	Before I went on work experience I was pleased with my placement.	67	28	3	2
5	I felt well prepared for my work experience.	57	42	1	0
6	The Health and Safety briefing was useful.	22	40	17	7
7	I knew what I wanted to achieve on my placement.	47	50	3	0
8	The preplacement interview helped me to feel more confident.	42	53	3	2

9 I knew what behaviour and attitude I should have during work experience.	82	18	0	0
10 The employer briefed me well before the placement.	46	42	8	4
11 The employer had put together a programme for me to follow.	34	30	18	10
12 Each task was carefully explained to me.	59	38	3	0
13. I was kept busy with a good range of things to do.	51	40	6	2
14 The rest of the staff made me feel welcome and part of the team.	81	13	6	1
15 I enjoyed my work experience.	74	15	8	3
16 If I had a problem there was help available.	69	28	3	0
17 I learnt a lot about myself from work experience.	38	43	14	6
18 I fulfilled my aims.	44	41	8	7
19 I would recommend this placement to someone else.	61	30	7	2
20 I feel more self-confident as a result of work experience.	48	47	3	2
21 I learnt a lot about other people and the jobs they do.	51	44	3	2
22 Work experience has motivated me to do the best that I can in my school work.	35	55	7	3
23 The employer talked to me about how well I did.	47	47	3	3

Action points resulting from the questionnaire responses were:

- to give support to employers who provided a less effective programme in order to improve the quality of the placement for next year

- to ensure that ongoing feedback is given by employers via staff visits during the placement.

In this example a great deal of data is generated. The number of questions could be reduced significantly to make it fit for your purpose. In this example, the school in question has used the same evaluative questionnaire for four years. This provides continuing quality control and allows comparisons to be drawn and trends to be identified. If issues were raised about a placement the careers coordinator talked to the pupil and the following year visited the employer before using the placement again. Sometimes issues were raised about a particular tutor group and the support they received. This identified a development need for the tutor.

Pupils enjoyed completing the questionnaire. Having one's opinion sought and taken seriously is a boost to self-esteem. Results were shared with the pupils, again showing that their input was valued.

This model for data generation could be adapted for any aspect of careers education. It is important to prioritise the use of evaluative questionnaires as they are time-consuming to process and analyse. It is important to ensure that the results generated will be used to celebrate good practice and to improve the teaching and learning in less good areas.

Classroom observation

Classroom observation can be a powerful tool for self-assessment but it can be easily mishandled with detrimental results. Be very clear about the purpose of classroom observation, such as:

- peer observation, to share good practice and to learn from each other

- team-leader observation, to gather good practice for cascading and to identify coaching needs within the team

- team-leader monitoring, with short periods of observation as 'an open-door policy' to monitor that the team is delivering the curriculum in an appropriate way (this identifies mavericks who are doing their own thing)

- team teaching, where one or two people take a leading role for a whole year group with the other members of the team in a supportive role. This models good practice effectively.

Once the purpose of the observation is clear, the appropriate method can be selected. There must be an atmosphere of mutual trust and collaboration before a period of observation begins. The purpose of the observation must be shared within the team and a common understanding achieved, otherwise it may lead to friction. Make the outcomes explicit, identifying the benefits. Make sure that, after the observation, there is proper feedback and follow-through. Action points must be identified with the appropriate support and time scale. Self-evaluative observation within a team is not about making judgements but about improving teaching and learning.

Evaluative meetings

This is the opportunity for a team to discuss the outcomes from the other forms of self-evaluation, to share what is working well, and to agree strategies for improving aspects that are going less well. Meetings should not be about giving information but about professional learning. This could either be through 'modelling workshops' where the teachers are led through the processes of an activity, or through evaluative workshops. Evaluative workshops must be planned into a yearly cycle of self-evaluation. The improvement must be ongoing, not just coming at the end the year or at the end of an event. Self-evaluation is about catching things as they start to happen, and taking avoidance action to prevent catastrophes. In the example of work experience, evaluation points must be put into the action plan. It is useful to have identified quality indicators as markers against which to make judgements, such as how many pupils should be placed by when.

Improving teaching and learning

Self-evaluation must result in action. It is interesting to analyse and point out shortfalls but the impact is made when there is a change in teaching and learning. Self-evaluation is only effective if it is used to bring about change that improves what takes place both within the classroom and beyond. It must improve the teachers' self awareness and through this their teaching abilities. It must improve standards across a team and it must provide a voice for change within the school. The ultimate goal is a consistently high standard of teaching and learning across a team that improves the life chances of young people.

The pupil perspective

Self-evaluation must empower pupils to become reflective learners. It must lead on to pupils being shown how to improve. A reflective pupil must have the support and guidance to enable them to make changes in their practice and they must know what they are aiming for. The following are some strategies for improvement.

Modelling by teachers or peers

In careers education it is useful to use personal experience as a model, but this must not be ad hoc; it must be planned and thought through. For example, if you are describing an achievement you have made in order to identify skills and qualities that you possess, you may not find it easy to think of a good example on the spur of the moment. You need to work out in advance the examples you will use.

Use of exemplars

Keep good examples of pupils' work to set high expectations, e.g. excellent Progress Files, outstanding personal statements, a collation of positive employer reports. If a task is to complete a self-assessment audit of skills, then model the first few to show the thought processes behind making a decision. Invest in a digital camera and take photos of pupils on work experience or enterprise days and use these for displays with incisive quotes. This sets high standards and expectations, and helps pupils to formulate in their own minds how to achieve their best.

Formative marking

Written work must have a purpose that is shared by pupil and teacher. If the outcome is to be meaningful then formative guidance on how to improve must be given. It is all too easy for PSHE and careers work to be put in a folder in the tutor room only to be binned when folders are tidied at the end of the year. If the purpose of writing is to coach in skills, such as writing a targeted CV, then there is a recognisable end product that needs to be reworked and improved. Rationalise the written work and spend quality time giving formative feedback. However, you need to be discriminating. You are not telling your team to mark all careers work: that would understandably lead to resentment. By targeting the guidance you are reducing the work load but ensuring that the work is meaningful. Formative guidance does not need to be written; it can be given orally during an activity, but encourage pupils to leave a lot of white space so that they can record your advice for future reference.

Development of self-questioning techniques

It is important to give pupils self-checking techniques. This could be a series of questions to apply to every piece of work, e.g. Is this my best work? What could I improve? Does my written work flow? Is the purpose of the work made clear in the content? Have I used a good logical structure? Have I used appropriate terminology? Pupils need support in the early stages of self-checking but it soon becomes second nature, and they develop a feeling of pride in producing their highest standard of work.

The teacher perspective

This is a difficult area. In theory, being a self-reflective practitioner leads to an improvement in classroom practice. However, it is hard to get the balance right in recognising strengths and making changes to improve weaknesses. It is very easy to criticise yourself after every lesson because one aspect of it was not spot on.

However, it is not possible to deliver the perfect lesson because pupils are diverse in their skills, abilities and learning styles, and the baggage they bring from the previous lesson, and from home life and peer dynamics. We need to be self-reflective without being over-critical of our imperfections.

When, through self-evaluation, you have identified some areas for improvement, what should happen next? Here are some ideas.

- Use peer observation with a critical friend. Ask a colleague to watch you teach, agreeing to focus on one of your strengths and one of your weaknesses. Ask for feedback and ideas for improvement. Observe your colleague teach using the same focus. Can any strategies be identified that you could try in your classroom?

- Many schools have a forum for sharing good practice where colleagues are nominated experts in certain fields, e.g. questioning techniques. Use peer support to plan a lesson together focusing on the identified area. Deliver the lesson, either being observed or videoed. Ask for feedback and coaching.

- Informal networking can be very productive. Ask colleagues whom you trust what they do that works well for them. If you gather enough ideas there is usually one that you feel comfortable with.

- Find out from the LEA if there is a designated Advanced Skills Teacher in your area. They should be able to offer support.

- Find a good book by a practitioner in your field and look for inspiration.

- Don't be afraid to try new things and ask for pupils' feedback.

The team perspective

If self-evaluation of your team raises issues that need to be addressed, proceed carefully and gradually. Hearts and minds need to be won before you wade in. As a leader you need to provide vision. The golden rule is that you need, first, to be clear in your own mind about where you want the team to be.

Careers education is unlikely to be high on teachers' agenda as they have many other roles and priorities. By using self-evaluation specific to careers the profile of careers is immediately raised. It will be your vision that leads the team forward. Self-evaluation is a tool for bringing together a group of disparate people and establishing a shared vision, and if you are clear in your ultimate goals then others will follow.

The school perspective

If you become skilled in what you do, then you will find your advice being sought on whole-school issues to raise standards across the board. You will have a way into many departments by having a team that represents a good cross section of the teaching staff. Examples that are used in careers will soon be modelled across the school.

You are establishing good practice to maximise learning within the classroom. This applies to all aspects of a good school. Publicise what you do and tell key people about it. Use other forums to share examples of what you are doing, e.g. heads of faculty meetings, heads of year meetings.

Summary

Effective and thorough self-evaluation can considerably increase teachers' and pupils' awareness of the learning that takes place. It encourages self-reflection and improvement which in turn accelerates learning. Improving careers education improves pupil motivation and leads to rising attainment across all subject areas.

Chapter 4
CHANGING CAREERS

- The current context

- Why is change necessary in schools?

- The benefits of change

- How to establish your starting point

- Planning for change

- Bringing about change

- Summary

The current context

Many current initiatives in careers education make this the right time for change in the curriculum. Careers education is about empowering pupils to make informed decisions about their education and their career choices beyond school and college. Pupils are now given the flexibility to choose their individual path at 14, and therefore need the knowledge and skills to make the choices that are most appropriate for them.

Finding your way through the overwhelming number of initiatives and directives can be a daunting prospect for even the most experienced careers coordinator. Many careers coordinators and senior managers cope by simply putting publications away in a cupboard and carrying on as before. A better strategy is to grasp the essence of the initiatives and embrace what is good, i.e. what will help young people to increase their life chances. Initiatives which you do not think will have any impact for young people may be safely ignored.

The following initiatives all have the same overall aim and usefully intertwine.

- Framework for Careers Education 11–19: advisory guidelines from September 2003

- Work-related learning for all 14–19 year olds: statutory from September 2004

- Careers Education in years 7 and 8: statutory from September 2004

- Individual Learning Plans for year 9 pupils: advisory guidelines from September 2004

- Framework for Citizenship: statutory from September 2002

- Framework for PSHE: advisory guidelines from September 2002

- A Progress File system: statutory from September 2004

- Personal development curriculum: QCA advisory guidelines from September 2004

Why is change necessary in schools?

These initiatives offer positive change, providing guidelines that will give structure, coherence and progression to the careers package. There is now no excuse for simply photocopying the nearest relevant resource without thinking where it fits into a programme or what pupils are supposed to be learning. There is now a sequence to follow which builds upon prior learning. This makes delivery of a careers programme more effective, by combining careers with other subject areas. The work-related learning framework also provides a context for delivering various areas of the curriculum. All this exposure will be good for pupils, particularly if seen as one overall package, which embraces choice and flexibility.

The Individual Learning Plan formalises the decisions made and ensures that they are based upon a long-term view of where the individual wants to be heading. Progress File pulls all aspects of the individual's self-development learning together to ensure that every pupil can see the links. These and other developments put the pupil firmly in control of their own future.

Change is necessary in schools to prepare pupils for the world of work. They will need to be able to embrace constant change, without suffering from anxiety and stress, as work patterns and technologies continue to evolve. Workers will need transferable skills, flexibility, adaptability and the confidence to rise to new challenges. They should not waste valuable time out of the work force by changing courses during post-16 study and higher education, or by dropping out of the system altogether.

In some schools careers programmes have been squeezed out of the curriculum to make more time for other subject areas. This may be because the benefits of careers education to the school league tables were not made explicit. In these circumstances the frameworks and statutory requirements can act as a good lever for ensuring that the careers education provision is reinstated. If curriculum time is not made available then other models need to be considered.

In other schools it is a good time to reinvigorate existing careers education. Most schools have excellent examples of good practice. Our purpose is to keep what is excellent, revamp what is good, and identify what is poor so that it can be taught in a new and exciting way, all the time asking if what you are doing is increasing the life chances of young people. It is not always about working harder, but about working differently to increase the impact.

The benefits of change

You may need to spell out to senior management teams the benefits of bringing about change in careers education. With the push for change coming from external agents now is a good time to argue for the benefits of change and for the way forward being led by someone from within the school. The motivation for change is not the external forces, but that we think it is a good thing to do, for pupils, teachers, and the school.

Benefits to the teacher

Teachers are learners. What motivates teachers to learn is no different to what motivates children. People of any age are more positive about all aspects of their life if they are learning. Merits, house points, raffle tickets or prizes do not motivate pupils to learn. The really motivational reward is the learning itself and the recognition of the learning by someone else.

It is no different with adults. Professional learning is necessary to prevent stagnation. Many experienced teachers who have not been given professional development opportunities have become disillusioned and demotivated. With change comes the need for professional learning. This change must be planned, supported and recognised in order to prevent teachers feeling overwhelmed and unsure of how to change to deliver new initiatives. With a good structure for professional development in place, teachers are motivated to perform better.

Careers education is often delivered by a high proportion of teachers in a school, i.e. the tutors. If this is the case then it can appear a daunting task to bring about change. If, however, the changes bring about professional development for the tutors, then it is more likely to have successful outcomes. Use careers education as a vehicle in which to deliver excellent teaching and learning using pedagogy that is relevant to all subject areas. Careers can become a model for other subject areas to follow. You are more likely to engage teachers who are not dedicated to careers education if the skills that you are modelling are transferable to their other teaching areas. Change in careers education will help teachers to learn professionally.

Benefits to pupils

If pupils' learning goals are clear then they are more likely to achieve them. Goals should be realistic but challenging. Pupils need a sequence of small steps to get them to their end point. The changes in careers education facilitate this approach, and should motivate pupils to achieve more, not merely in terms of exam performance but, just as importantly, in self-development. The development of self-awareness and empathy is crucial to success in work. With a successfully coherent, progressive, linked, individualised programme, pupils should be leaving school with clear direction and the skills necessary to put their plans into action.

Benefits to the school

Benefits to teachers and to pupils will bring direct benefits to the school. Attainment will go up, with more pupils achieving added value in more subject areas. Pupils will be more self-managing, which reduces discipline issues. Teachers will be more aware of effective teaching and learning; this increases motivation and makes the time in the classroom more rewarding. Shared change in an institution brings about collaborative working which, in itself, leads to greater professional learning.

How to establish your starting point

Establishing the base line of where your institution currently stands is vital to start the process of change. It helps you to identify strengths and weaknesses which can then be used to schedule the plan of change.

There are many self-assessment tools available to help you establish a starting point. There are local quality frameworks which provide audit materials. These are put into manageable categories such as work experience, resources, individual guidance, the taught curriculum, etc. If your local Connexions partnership does not have its own quality award then there are national examples available, for instance one on the CEGNET website (www.cegnet.com).

Although these processes can be lengthy they are thorough. You should be able to enlist the help of a CEG support teacher to provide help and guidance if needed. You may find such audits are rather blunt tools with which to evaluate the situation in your school, your response to each statement being a subjective one. However, it is the discussion that follows an audit exercise that is the most valuable part, as it gives the opportunity to explore the issues and to justify the responses. For useful discussions to happen you need a critical friend or line manager who understands the principles of careers education and has an overview of whole school procedures.

An alternative way to establish where you are is to use the Ofsted standards which explore five components of careers education:

- careers education within the curriculum: 11-19 framework implementation, curriculum planning and coordination

- planning and recording of achievement and work-related activity

- work experience

- access to individual guidance and support

- access to careers information.

For each category identify your school's strengths and weaknesses. You may need to collect evidence, or present evidence, to make the process less subjective. You will need to know that your perception is accurate, in order to establish whether what you set out to be delivered is being delivered with quality and consistency to each pupil.

The type of evidence to look for when establishing the base line is:

- analysis of pupils' work – Progress Files, work experience log books, lesson outcomes, guidance interview accounts

- talking with pupils – focused discussion groups, based on, for example, work experience, the Real Game, guidance interviews, options

- lesson observation

- partnership with parents

- staff interviews

- self-evaluation.

The key outcomes of such a review should be to identify:

- the strengths

- the issues

- the evidence

- the action needed.

Planning for change

The outcomes of the audit should be reported and shared with the senior management team. It is vital to engage them at an early stage because you will need their support to bring about changes at a whole-school level. Part of this should be agreeing a timescale over which to plan. In most schools there will be a planning cycle leading into a whole-school development plan (or improvement plan or transformation plan depending on which stage your school is at) on which it would make sense to 'piggyback'. There is no point in duplicating work. If this is the case then you may have a pro forma to which you must work. If you do not, then you should use sections such as:

- current context: where are we now?

- where careers education will be in three years' time (or whatever the agreed timescale is)

- action, specific with named individuals and dates

- impact: what difference the change will make to pupils

- monitoring: ongoing quality indicators that check the progress made

- evaluation, providing opportunities for continuing improvement and adjustment.

Start by listing in priority order the areas that need to be changed. The top priority may not be the greatest need but may be small tasks that are easy to fix and have instant impact. You may wish to plan more time-consuming tasks for the second half of the summer term. You will need to work in small manageable steps: remember it is a marathon not a sprint. Secondly, break down each area into specific tasks; identify who is best placed to carry out each task and check they are willing. Agree a realistic timescale.

Monitoring is crucial to success but is sometimes overlooked. Put progress checkpoints into the plan. These may be termly meetings or less formal chats at which you can share what progress has been made, but put an outcome and a date for these checkpoints in the plan. Evaluation will assess the quality of the change and check the effectiveness. This should tie in with self-evaluation processes.

Once you have produced the plan, issue it as a draft for checking by all the key players. Ask for feedback and give a date by which you need to receive it. This gives people the opportunity to fine-tune their areas of responsibility and to state any objections.

Bringing about change

Writing a development plan does not in itself bring about change. It is easy to file a plan and not look at it again until the next review cycle the following year. It is a cliché, but the plan must be a working document that provides the structure to lead you through the process. You should have it in a prominent place and cross out sections as they are completed.

To make the change effective you will not be working in isolation but with several different people. Your job is to motivate these people to carry out their part of the plan within the agreed timescale.

Ten tips for bringing about successful change

- Lead by example: carry out what you have agreed to do and share it with your colleagues.

- Engage all working partners at an early stage so that they own the plan.

- Ask people's advice on what to do and make sure you include the best of it to show that their opinions are valued.

- Show interest in progress made by others: this can be time-consuming but gives everyone the opportunity to discuss with you what they are doing.

- Offer ongoing support.

- Celebrate achievement, recognise what has been done, and give praise publicly; keep a log of ephemeral evaluation (feedback which has been given orally and will be lost unless written down) which can be motivational at review meetings.

- Thank people individually for what they have done. Verbal appreciation is important but written thanks shows you have taken the time to give it, and it can also be used for the teacher's own professional development portfolio.

- If someone is reluctant to make a start then suggest a collaboration in which you will work on the first stages with them.

- A couple of weeks before monitoring points, have informal chats about 'how things are going'. This brings the tasks back to the forefront of people's minds with sufficient time to do some work if necessary.

- Make sure that hard work and good work is recognised by senior managers as well as by you.

If you follow these tips, you will be managing the change effectively. Make sure all work done is part of the overall plan so that all parties are working towards the same ends. You do not want colleagues investing time and energy on their own versions of things without the context of the big picture. This can lead to disengagement.

Summary

Carry out an assessment of where the school is at with its careers provision; enlist help with this if you need it. Identify strengths and weaknesses and prioritise areas to work on. Get colleagues on board at an early stage to give ownership and a collegiate approach. Produce a useful development plan, something that will guide and help you. Plan small achievable tasks that can be quickly accomplished. Set realistic timescales and monitor progress. Recognise what has been done and celebrate success.

Chapter 5
MOTIVATIONAL MOVES

- Identifying reluctant colleagues

- Strategies for motivating colleagues

- Improving consistency

- Summary

Introduction

To be successful in implementing change you will need to engage the support of all stake holders. In addition you will be relying on other colleagues to teach careers. Many will respond well and always do their best to deliver engaging lessons with a high degree of learning taking place. On the other hand, some colleagues may have limited interest, see careers as low priority, have poor understanding, and be reluctant to change. They may feel threatened when presented with new ways of working because it moves them out of their comfort zone.

Identifying reluctant colleagues

There are at least five categories of colleagues and most of them will not be helpful to your cause unless handled with diplomacy. They are the people who:

- say, 'I would help but I'm too busy with my own responsibilities'

- say, 'yes' to everything, get overloaded with work, and are unable to deliver the goods

- say they will do something for you but always have an excuse as to why they have not been able to, or they simply forget about it

- say 'It's against union guidelines; my time is for marking and preparation only'

- offer support because they see it as advancement of their own career

- offer support because they believe in what you are doing and want to help, or you have previously built up an atmosphere of trust when they have worked with you.

Only colleagues in the last two categories will help you and work with you. The others are all blockers in their own particular way. Many colleagues may well be hostile to change. You must anticipate what colleagues' reactions will be when you put proposals forward. You do not want to find yourself putting your plan forward and have verbal or non-verbal opposition in public. It is obviously uncomfortable when a colleague challenges you in a way intended to undermine you in a public forum with phrases such as 'Why are we doing this?' or 'I can't see how this would work' or 'We tried this 20 years ago and it didn't work then'. It is equally off-putting when a colleague crosses their arms, leans back in their chair and looks out of the window, shaking their head. The biggest nightmare is having several people using various destructive strategies at the same time.

Strategies for motivating colleagues

Once you have established your own values and vision for change you are in a strong position to communicate these and to give consistent messages. They should be backed up by your own actions, otherwise there will be discord between what you say and what you do. Discord leads to misunderstanding and mistrust. We can all think of colleagues who preach one thing and practise another. When this happens their leadership begins to collapse because they will not be followed.

The most positive thing that you can do is to recognise strengths of colleagues and praise them for what they do well. It is vital also to remember to thank people when they have put themselves out for you or for others. Nobody likes to be taken for granted. People will want to work with you if they like and respect you and this means leading by example and not letting people down. Only commit to doing something if you can deliver. If you let somebody down then they have little or no incentive to get things right for you.

There are several things that you can do to ensure that meetings run smoothly. You must plan carefully and anticipate. You need to know your colleagues and understand them well. Here are some things that you can try.

- Be clear in your own mind what you want to say and how you want to introduce something new.

- Make sure you can explain why you are introducing the changes and how you are going to make the task manageable.

- Make sure written proposals are clear and concise; get someone to check it for you to iron out any wrinkles.

- Identify the benefits to both pupils and staff and be ready to communicate them.

- Anticipate arguments against your proposal and have facts and figures to counter them.

- Carry out pilot samples to provide evidence of your idea working in practice.

- Flatter your most stubborn blocker by asking them to work with you on the pilot study and to present the findings to the rest of the team.

- Share your plans with like-minded colleagues who will support you during the meeting, so creating the critical mass in agreement with the changes that you are trying to implement.

- Show individual colleagues your proposal in early draft stages and ask for their advice, saying that you value their opinion. Take some of their suggestions on board and give them credit for their ideas in the introductory meeting, thus implying their support.

- Try to create time for colleagues to carry out the work by seeking funding, cover arrangements or having time protected from invigilation or cover during exam periods.

- Organise some INSET training with an expert from outside the school who has evidence that your proposals have been tried and tested in other similar schools and found to work.

In your introductory meeting make sure that you have your line manager, with whom you have been working closely, present to give support and pull rank if necessary. She/he should also be useful in adding the whole-school perspective and fielding questions. If a meeting or an individual conversation with a colleague begins to turn negative, suggest a postponement to allow time to explore the issues and to come up with alternative strategies. Do not allow a negative conversation to dominate a meeting as this only wastes valuable time. If you are challenged directly, do not try to pull rank by saying, 'This is not the time or place for this conversation.' This merely offends colleagues and undermines the collegiate style of working that you need. Instead, put forward the positive aspects of the points you are making in a clear and succinct way, remaining calm and thoughtful.

Improving consistency

There is a potential conflict of responsibilities between the head of year leading the year team and the careers coordinator who has responsibility for the impact of the learning for careers in the classroom. In particular it will not be the responsibility of the careers coordinator to implement systems to improve consistency across year teams. It is therefore vitally important for the head of year and careers coordinator to discuss pedagogy and leadership so that there is a common understanding. Year-team meetings (or the like) should be developmental and not, as in many schools, administrative. A team meeting should be an opportunity for the professional coaching of colleagues and a contribution to their continued professional development.

Here are some strategies that can be used to help consistency of delivery of careers education. The careers coordinator should work in a collegiate way with the team leader to decide which strategies would work well with the team in question.

INSET session for all heads of year

This could also be run for a team with responsibility for managing PSHE and citizenship, in conjunction with the senior manager with responsibility for self-development, PSHE and citizenship. The aim is to reach a common understanding about what a lesson plan should contain, how to improve the learning outcomes, how to ensure that three-part lessons are in place, how to evaluate the effectiveness of the learning, etc. The summer term is a good time for this training in preparation for the following academic year. It is a golden opportunity to improve understanding and consistency within the leadership team. Even if true consistency is not achieved, the professional discussions should cause the leaders to reassess their understanding of pedagogy.

Identifying skills within the team

In any team there will be a mixture of people with different strengths and skills. It is important to recognise these and divide up responsibilities accordingly. Some team members will generate good ideas, some will turn these into practical terms, some will write lesson plans and some will find resources.

Buddy system

Develop a buddy system in a year team where tutors who complement each other are paired up for mentoring. This system can encourage joint planning with occasions for team teaching or lesson observations.

Model activities for colleagues

Modelling activities is more effective than handing colleagues written instructions. There will be very little transfer of information, and a loss of impact in the classroom, unless people experience something directly. Meetings can be run as a model lesson with a starter activity, shared learning outcomes and shortened versions of pupil activities for tutors to carry out. This should be followed with the opportunity for review and reflection. If tutors try something out and then discuss how to improve it, there will be more ownership and tutors will approach the lesson with a greater degree of confidence.

Video clips of careers activities within the classroom

If a teacher on the team is particularly good at starter activities, video a few activities and use the clips within team meetings to stimulate discussion about what works well. This is a more cost-effective way of sharing experiences than lesson observations. Additionally, the person recorded will learn a great deal about themselves by watching themselves on video. The subtleties and dynamics that are lost during the lesson can be picked out much more easily when viewing the video. This technique can also be used if someone is struggling and needs some coaching and advice.

Lesson observations

Observations of lessons by the team leader or careers coordinator may be highly effective for improving the impact within the classroom, therefore accelerating the learning of the pupils. This tool only works well if the findings are used as a basis for developmental work. The observation itself will not help the deliverer; it is the quality of the feedback and resulting professional dialogue that is important. This should be done as part of the self-evaluation framework. Good practice should be shared with the team and areas for development should be highlighted and addressed. This strategy is highly time-consuming when colleagues need support. Therefore the senior leadership team must understand the importance of this work and be committed to it as a way to school improvement. Pairs of people will need to be protected from cover to allow the professional dialogue to happen. The delivery in the classroom will not change if the lesson observation is not followed through, as often happens with the conflicting pressures of day-to-day teaching.

Whole year-group sessions

Running sessions for a year group of pupils, with tutors in a supportive role, is another modelling tool. When you have sessions for the whole year group or an assembly it presents a good opportunity for showing teaching and learning techniques.

Summary

Careers teaching may not be high on colleagues' agenda. However well set up lesson activities are, it is the transfer of ways of effective teaching that is important. Colleagues will only give careers a high priority if they can see the value of it and if there are direct benefits to them. It is up to the careers coordinator to work with other middle and senior managers to provide leadership that improves the effectiveness of teaching and learning in the classroom. This will only happen if colleagues are motivated.

Chapter 6
EMOTIONALLY INTELLIGENT CAREERS

- What is emotional intelligence?

- Recognising emotional intelligence

- How does emotional intelligence relate to careers education?

- Teaching careers in an emotionally intelligent way

- Summary

What is emotional intelligence?

Emotional intelligence is an important element in activating the power of learning. Learning is not just about achieving learning outcomes: it is about the processes and steps to get there. Learning involves pupils being empowered to become independent thinkers and decision makers. Emotional intelligence brings an enhanced awareness of one's own emotions and those of others. Emotions can be used productively to lead to strong and effective working relationships. Emotional intelligence helps us to learn from failure and use this learning to advance along the next steps.

Many schools are working towards an emotionally aware curriculum. This will only succeed when teachers are themselves emotionally intelligent because emotional intelligence is about people and their interactions, which is part of the hidden school curriculum. Teachers' values, attitudes and behaviour can produce a classroom atmosphere that either hinders emotional development or engenders it. Emotional intelligence can be taught and can be fostered within an organisation. It must be present at all levels, in relationships between teachers, between teachers and pupils, and amongst pupils themselves.

Recognising emotional intelligence

Key words for an emotionally intelligent classroom are:

belonging, concern, consideration, creativity, empathy, energy, flexibility, honesty, impact, integrity, intuition, leadership, listening, motivation, negotiation, openness, reflection, respect, self-belief, self-worth, sensitivity, shared values, tolerance, trust.

For an un-emotionally intelligent classroom key words are:

anger, anti-social behaviour, boredom, conflict, destruction, frustration, humiliation, intolerance, inconsiderateness, isolation, low self-esteem, marginalisation, mistrust, ridicule, sabotage.

With the first group come effective learning and success; with the second come halted learning and low success.

It is easy to think of words to describe the emotionally aware classroom or school. The difficulty lies in achieving the cultural shift needed to make this a reality when the leaders are adults with established behaviours and beliefs. The answer lies in planning a taught curriculum that allows for emotional development, and modelling emotional practice throughout all layers of the school. Meetings and adult interactions should use behaviours described in the first word list. Positive practice should be encouraged, recognised and praised within the classroom, with both staff and pupils.

Pupils are quick to recognise the link between emotional intelligence and effective learning. A year 10 tutor group was asked to complete the sentence, 'A good teacher is someone who . . . ' Here is a representative sample of their replies.

A good teacher is someone who…

'is a good talker as well as a good listener'

'has fun but you learn a lot'

'does lots of different activities'

'is humorous in the lesson – I think this helps pupils learn'

'doesn't have a go at you all the time but takes time to understand you'

'listens to you when you have a problem'

'you can talk to'

'will give you advice and will talk to you and listen to you'

'makes things fun – a bit laid back'

'gets along with the class – funny but strict'

'understands – doesn't shout – explains stuff in an easy way'

'listens to your problems if you don't understand something'.

These responses are all based on emotional intelligence. The replies are not about how well knowledge is imparted but about the pupils' relationships and interactions with the teacher. Unless the relationship is right, effective learning will not take place. This must be true of teacher-to-pupil and pupil-to-pupil interactions.

Evidence of emotional intelligence can be sought during self-evaluative processes, and can form the focus of a review. Many people struggle to quantify the degree to which a lesson, teacher or pupil can be assessed as being emotionally intelligent. Often it is about an atmosphere and not something tangible. The judgement is often instinctive, a gut feeling, which makes it difficult to gather evidence. It is often easier to establish when a situation is *not* managed in an emotionally intelligent way and pupils or staff are literally and figuratively backed into a corner. Often, upon reflection the situation could have been diffused or eased with timely interjections, e.g. the use of humour.

Five examples of emotionally intelligent behaviour

- If a pupil has not completed their homework, instead of issuing a detention, ask the pupil why the homework has not been completed. Offer support to get the work done and negotiate a new deadline.

- If teasing by one pupil of another has resulted in tears, instead of punishing the teaser, meet with them both so that the upset party can express their feelings in a secure environment. Get the teaser to explain why and how they have upset the other person, and ask how they would deal with the situation differently the next time.

- Let pupils make the decisions when they ask what to do next. Instead of giving them the answer put it back to them: 'What do you think you should do next?'

- Encourage democratic processes that include all opinions. For example, in group work ask each member of the group to write down or say what the next step should be, and then all vote on the most appropriate action. This prevents the dominant person bulldozing through a task, leaving others feeling frustrated.

- A tutor group were asked to produce a newspaper about themselves. Initially they chose cliquey photographs and captions that clearly excluded some members of the group. After discussion the same people realised what they had done, and that some members of the class clearly felt left out. They reworked the paper using photographs that included everybody with captions that shared humour without ridicule.

When emotional intelligence is apparent in a classroom, it should be recognised and praised.

How does emotional intelligence relate to careers education?

Emotional intelligence is as important as academic qualifications. A person with a high level of self-awareness is more likely to relate well to other people and to form meaningful relationships. This is the basis of human happiness. Someone with secure home and working relationships is going to be more fulfilled and successful in all aspects of their lives. They are therefore less likely to drop out of society.

Our role in careers education is to equip people with the skills for lifelong learning to enable them to succeed in further study and work. Part of this must be to allow the development and awareness of emotional skills. Personal and social development is as important as the academic curriculum; without the first the second will be irrelevant. Educators are increasingly aware that learning is by serendipity: it is a haphazard process and will only occur if the learner is emotionally receptive.

The crucial element is not so much the knowledge that is taught but how the learner receives it, processes it and interacts with others around them.

The development of skills in personal development and social interaction are therefore the key to equipping young people with the self-awareness and emotional intelligence they need to become fulfilled and happy adults who continue to learn throughout their life. The careers curriculum is not about discrete learning outcomes that can be ticked off, but about growing as a person. It is not about delivering knowledge but about emotional development. If you ask a pupil what they have learnt in careers lessons they will probably reply, 'Nothing.' If you ask what they have learnt about themselves you are likely to get a more constructive and self-aware answer. As a year 10 pupil, returning from work experience, put it: 'I didn't learn much about work but I look at myself in a completely different way now. I am now a person who can confidently go after the job I want. I am determined to succeed'.

She could not explain what had happened to her in terms of new skills, but it is evident that her self-esteem had grown, she had found a positive direction, and higher goals had been set for her. This cannot be measured but it can be seen.

Emotional development is apparent throughout the careers framework. From KS3 there are, for example, the following words: self-confidence, positive self-image, reflection, goals, views, decision making, and values. Similar words appear in the

PSHE and citizenship framework: active participation is vital; positive behaviours lead to success and reward; negative behaviours are destructive. Our role as educators and parents is to encourage 'buying in' rather than 'opting out' from the earliest age possible.

A careers education package in secondary school will not alone achieve emotional growth in all pupils. Active citizenship will not automatically occur by participation in careers lessons. The role of careers education is to develop a positive sense of self. This, of course, is the goal of all educators, but careers education has the luxury of having these outcomes stated in the Framework: it is the content to be delivered. It is vital therefore to model emotionally aware behaviours in all careers sessions and activities.

Teaching careers in an emotionally intelligent way

It is critical to examine values when negotiating the model of delivery of careers education. Having an atmosphere of trust between the teacher and the pupils is a crucial value for an emotionally intelligent classroom. This is more likely to be achieved if the teacher already has a relationship with the group, for example, as their tutor. If a PSHE team delivers careers without knowing the pupils then it is unrealistic to expect emotional growth. Positive relationships are vital to success. This is an argument for pupils choosing which tutor they wish to have, one whom they respect and trust and who can help them to grow as people. All too often we expect tutors to step into tutor groups half way through their school career and have an instant rapport and trust. But trust is built through time and shared experiences. It cannot be imposed by taking over a tutor group in year 10 and expecting that bond to exist readymade.

So what can be done? Emotionally intelligent behaviours can be encouraged through careers lessons. Lesson plans can contain learning outcomes for emotional development. The processes should be modelled with the teachers who are delivering the lessons during training sessions.

Ten ideas for emotional intelligence in careers lessons

Who am I?

This is suitable for all key stages as part of a self-awareness programme. Each pupil is asked to think of between five and ten emotional outcomes that they want for their lives, e.g. happiness, trustworthy friends, belonging, security, etc. Once the list is drawn up the pupil is asked to think of a metaphor for their life that encompasses these emotions, such as a bear curled up in a cosy cave, a footballer scoring a triumphant goal, etc. They should think about how they want it to look, sound and feel, and about the colours that they want it to be. They draw and colour the metaphor with their words placed around it.

Activity review

This can be used after any activity in which the aim has been to work as a team to solve a problem, e.g. producing a class newspaper, deciding which charity to raise funds for, acting in work roles for work experience preparation, or enterprise activities. Pupils are asked to reflect upon how they feel at the end of a session by choosing the most appropriate statement for them. The statements are as follows:

- I feel happy.

- I feel gloomy.

- I feel confident.

- I feel anxious.

- I feel it was my fault.

- I feel successful.

This helps pupils to unpick why they are left feeling the way they do at the end of a session.

Managing difficult situations on work experience

This is part of the preparation for work experience. During work experience pupils will meet people who praise, value and support them; but they may also meet people who ridicule, humiliate and bully them. Being aware of the reasons for these responses can help them to come out of such an experience less damaged than they might otherwise be.

Thought shower the reasons why some people put down others. Remember in thought showering to accept all ideas without passing judgement, and then unpick afterwards. Responses may be things such as control, jealousy, feelings of insecurity, low self-esteem, feeling threatened, etc.

Discuss the outcomes and then ask pupils to think of an experience in which someone said or did something that really bothered or upset them. Ask: What was the person trying to achieve for themself? How did you respond in that situation? How could you have responded differently to leave yourself feeling less raw? What could you do if this occurs on work experience?

How do I see myself?

This can be another preparation activity for work experience. It is based on peer assessment for self-awareness and should be used before pupils present themselves to their work experience host on a preplacement interview.

Pupils are given 20 statements and they are asked to place themselves on a four-point scale for each where 1 is strongly agree, 2 is slightly agree, 3 is slightly disagree and 4 is strongly disagree. The statements relate to how they present themselves to others, e.g. 'I smile when I am introduced to someone new', 'I have good body posture', and 'I walk into a room confidently'.

Once they have graded themselves they do the same for a critical friend who is asked to be as honest as possible. At the end they compare and discuss the outcomes. This can be a delicate process if the self-perception does not agree with the perception of the critical friend. Positive factors should be used to boost self-esteem. Strategies need to be given to address weak areas that are identified.

Values into practice – a code of behaviour for work experience

This session is important in preparation for work experience. It can be run on the model of a class council, with a chairperson who collects all the suggestions and leads discussions.

The aim is for the tutor group to decide on ten golden rules for behaviour on work experience. To start they can be given an example of a placement that has gone horribly wrong in the past due to a pupil's actions. They should unpick what has gone wrong and propose actions that the pupil could have taken to avoid conflict.

From this each pupil writes down three suggestions for rules for good behaviour on work experience. These are then shared and voted on by each member of the tutor group. The ten golden rules can then be written into their log books or journals.

One-to-one interview preparation

This is suitable for all ages of pupils. To prepare for one-to-one interviews, academic mentoring, or discussions about learning plans, pupils are given a prompt sheet to complete. On it pupils are asked to describe their greatest ambition, identify their educational goal and, most importantly, describe any barriers that are preventing them from realising their ambitions. This then forms the basis of a discussion about why pupils may not be reaching their goals and what can be done to help them.

How others influence your decision making (KS4)

Having identified what a value is and thought showered some ideas, pupils carry out an exercise about their own values. This can be done by giving pupils ten statements of value on a bar graph and asking them to shade in the bar to the height that they hold that value.

Pupils then complete an influences wheel. They write around the spokes of the wheel all the people who have an influence on them, e.g. parents, named friends, tutor, personal adviser, brother, etc. For each person they write down one value that he or she holds in relation to education or work.

Pupils then reflect upon how their values coincide or conflict with the people who influence them. This exercise may throw up some issues which are difficult to resolve, e.g. if parents have different values to the pupil. Once in the open these issues can be discussed, which may relieve some of the tension and frustration that the pupil is feeling.

Raising self-esteem

This exercise is suitable for any age group and would be well placed before compiling personal statements or completing progress file activities. It works well in a group of about ten, so in a tutor group have three circles of people. One person from each group is sent out of the room. Each member of the group has to write down one positive thing about the pupil's character. A speaker is nominated to check that the statements are acceptable. The pupil returns to the room where the statements are read out by the speaker. They are strictly anonymous. The roles then change until, over a period of time, all pupils in the group have heard what others have to say about them.

Skills for employability and discrimination (KS4)

Give pupils a photograph of an icon of success, e.g. David Beckham. Pupils must write down what they think of him, as a person and as a footballer. Within the group there will be those who adore him and those who loathe him. The learning point is that every individual's opinion of David Beckham is based upon their image of him and upon their own value and belief system.

Pupils are then asked to put their own opinion to one side and consider the evidence for giving David Beckham a job: Would you employ him? In small groups pupils identify the skills, qualities and attributes that have made him successful, as well as any other contributory factors. This can be drawn up into a class collage about him using images and words to describe him.

The learning point is that, even if we have a set view of someone, then other people's opinions may differ because we are in some way comparing the person to ourselves and making a judgement which is not always accurate or based upon fact. In the workplace this can lead to discrimination if we do not respect other people's opinions.

Asking for help (KS3 and KS4)

As Big Ears said to Noddy, 'By all means try something yourself first, but if you get stuck it's best to ask someone to help you, otherwise you can end up in a terrible mess'. Knowing when and how to ask for help is a very important skill: it requires emotional intelligence in order to get a desired outcome. The following activity may be done in conjunction with identifying sources of help.

Pose some basic questions, e.g. Why do people help each other? Why might people not help someone else? Relate this then to their parents: When you want something, e.g. to go out, what do you do to get your own way? What can be learnt from this when asking for help?

Draw up a class checklist, e.g. be polite, smile, arrange a convenient time to see the person, be appreciative, be clear about what you want to find out, read other people's emotions, don't ask them if they appear stressed, etc. Pupils can then try out their new strategies and see if people are more responsive.

Summary

Developing emotional intelligence in the classroom is about doing something differently to change the way in which pupils learn. Pupils are in control of their emotions and are ready for learning by becoming more self-aware. Careers education provides an excellent opportunity for teaching emotional intelligence. The benefit is that pupils will be more successful by being aware of their goals and how to achieve them.

Chapter 7
PROGRESSIVE PLANNING

- Recognising progression

- Themes of progression in careers education

- Linking progression to learning theories

- Using progression in planning lesson sequences

- Summary

Recognising progression

Schools now have a statutory duty to provide pupils with a careers education programme from years 7 to 13. During these seven years of education there must be a progressive programme that builds upon prior learning, contributes to moral and spiritual growth of a pupil, and allows skills for employability to be recognised and developed. Within this programme is the promotion of personal and social development. The introduction of flexible learning pathways for 14-19 year olds makes it now more crucial than ever to prepare pupils to make informed choices.

Progression is crucial within a careers programme, since the programme covers such a wide time span, with pupils passing through many stages of cognitive and emotional development. A static programme which does not allow pupils to move forward will lead to them becoming disengaged and disenchanted with careers education.

Progression is built into the National Framework for Careers Education. There are three main themes: self-development, career exploration, and career management. These themes are common to the three key stages and are further subdivided into learning outcomes which link between the key stages. Although the areas of learning remain mostly the same there is inbuilt progression taking into account the prior learning.

Each key stage has a set of instructive words which allude to the progression required, and these must be taken into account when planning sequences of lessons and continuation of themes from one key stage to another.

At KS3 the instructive words are: undertake, use, recognise, respond, describe, identify, demonstrate and organise. There are particular activities in year 9 where the words change to 'make realistic and informed choices' and 'consider alternatives'. At KS4 the instructive words are cognitively more complex, e.g. review, reflect, explain, action plan, respond appropriately, select, understand and compare. The post-16 curriculum uses instructive words such as: make critical use, process effectively, justify, evaluate, take charge, improve, consider implications, obtain and manage.

The instructive words are based upon a hierarchical order system where the cognitive expectations are much higher as the themes move up through the key stages. This is based on Bloom's Taxonomy where families of words increase in the level of cognitive demand as they move down the taxonomical grouping. The words can be used to frame learning outcomes to build in progression.

Teachers and pupils must be familiar with the meaning of the words in order to increase the demand on the pupil and to challenge their thinking. All too often, even in post-16 teaching, a pupil fails to distinguish between describe, explain and compare and contrast. Pupils need to be coached in the use of these words from a very early stage as they traverse all curriculum areas.

Themes of progression in careers education

Within the three main themes there are foci which progress through all key stages. These are stated in the National Framework document:

Self-development

- use of self-assessments to allow target- and goal-setting
- use of self-assessment to identify areas for development
- developing skills needed to progress
- stereotyping
- influences

Career exploration

- identifying different meanings of the term 'work'
- changing world of work

- using careers information

- different career routes

- using other experiences of work

- understanding progression routes

Career management

- using decision-making techniques

- comparing options

- managing transitions including financial implications

- application procedures

- presenting themselves to others

Once the curriculum is broken down into these sixteen areas it becomes much more manageable and understandable.

Linking progression to learning theories

As mentioned in Chapter 1, there are many theories of learning which follow the same hierarchical sequence as the one outlined through use of instructive words in the Framework. For example, Gagne produces a theoretical framework based around the theory of 'conditions of learning'. In this Gagne suggests that learning tasks for intellectual skills can be organised into a sequence of increasing complexity: stimulus recognition, response generation, procedure following, use of terminology, discriminations, concept formation, rule application and problem solving.

This increasing complexity is mirrored in the Framework. At KS3 the instructive words of undertake, identify, describe, etc. are founded in the formative stages of following procedures and using terminology. It is not until KS4 that discrimination is encouraged by the use of words such as review, reflect and select. Rule application and problem solving is encouraged in the post-16 curriculum by the use of descriptors such as evaluate, consider implications and manage effectively.

There is a slight dichotomy when comparing the Framework with Piaget's theory of 'genetic epistemology'. Piaget relates cognitive development to stages in child development. However, he also says that the progression is not age-dependent: in any class there will be children at different stages of cognitive development, and some pupils will not reach the level of formal operations that involves abstractions.

If this is true then there are clear implications for curriculum planning. The progression in the framework is time-based and hierarchical as pupils move through the key stages. However, as explored in Chapter 1, pupils will not all progress at the same rate and some pupils during KS3 will be working at the level of formal operations and will need to be challenged in their thinking in order to progress. Other post-16 pupils will not reach this level of cognitive development and will still be operating at the concrete operational stage.

If we remove the boundaries constructed through the key stages and look instead at the individual and their progression, then the theories begin to complement the curriculum. The progression complements Bruner's constructivist theory in which learners construct new ideas or concepts based upon their prior knowledge and understanding. The teacher's role is to translate the new learning which is expected into a format which the learner can access because it relates to the learner's current state of understanding. The careers curriculum is a spiral where concepts are built up as they are revisited. This lends itself to progression, but it must be appreciated that the prior knowledge and understanding will be different for each pupil. Therefore there will be a range of expected learning within a class.

To facilitate the learning for all pupils, the conceptual levels must not be restricted to key stage. It is important to use differentiated learning outcomes which use hierarchical instructive words to encourage conceptual development. This will be crucial when careers is taught to a mixed ability tutor group since pupils will be at very different conceptual stages.

Using progression in planning lesson sequences

Progression should be at the centre of every lesson, with pupils developing their ideas and conceptual understanding. In addition, there must be progression in sequences of lessons. For example, preparation for option choices in year 9 may form a programme which spans a sequence of four lessons. During the lesson sequence every pupil would be expected to develop their understanding. The progression must be recognised and be used to plan a logical sequence of lessons rather than four discrete lessons which could be delivered in any order.

The first step in planning the sequence would be to identify the relevant learning outcomes from the Framework. In this example these would be the following.

- Demonstrate knowledge and understanding of the options open to them including opportunities provided through vocational options.

- Identify and use a variety of sources of careers information including ICT.

- Identify and access help and advice.

- Manage change and transition, giving consideration to longer term implications and the potential progression opportunities.

- Make realistic and informed choices of options available post-14.

- Consider alternatives and make changes in response to their successes and failures.

Before these outcomes can be achieved pupils would need to be aware of stereotypes in terms of the main influences in their lives and their preconceptions about their place in the world of work and society. They will have had a foundation of goal-setting and self-awareness development. This may form part of a programme earlier in the year or at the end of year 8.

The next step is to determine a logical progression in the concepts to be taught. Pupils cannot make informed choices before they are aware of the choices available to them. Here is a possible sequence of lessons.

Lesson 1

Pupils undertake an activity to determine their preferred learning style and relate the outcome to the KS4 courses on offer to them. The outcomes are recorded in the Progress File and, together with data, are used to help guide pupils towards the most appropriate courses on offer. Pupils should be aware of the different skills, level of ability and learning styles for each option choice. For example, a BTEC first diploma in performing arts may be offered as an alternative to GCSE drama. Which type of learner would be suited to each?

Lesson 2

Pupils draft two alternative sets of option choices and look at the progression routes available as a result of their choices. Pupils use ICT to explore job families that relate to their skills, qualifications gained and learning styles.

Lesson 3

Pupils undertake a simple decision-making technique, e.g. pros and cons or SWOT analysis, to explore which is the most appropriate route for them. Pupils identify what help they need before making the final decision, and they action plan how they are going to access this support.

Before the next lesson pupils should have a guidance conversation about their option choices. This would need to span a few weeks and could be with the tutor or a personal/careers adviser.

Lesson 4

Pupils produce a personal statement (or Individual Learning Plan) which includes their option choices, their reasons for decisions made, implications of these decisions, goal-setting for KS4, future career plans, etc. This record provides a summary of the learning that has taken place over the lesson sequence.

Within each lesson there should also be differentiation and progression. This will come about through the use of differentiated, sharp learning outcomes and through activities which are directed at the different levels of cognitive understanding.

Summary

Progression should be identified in the careers curriculum giving coherence between the key stages. The instructive words are hierarchical and they facilitate learning at different stages of cognitive development. Within each class there will be pupils at different levels of prior understanding. Instructive words should be used to differentiate learning outcomes to allow every individual to progress in their learning.

Chapter 8
JOINED-UP THINKING

- Linking careers to citizenship and PSHE

- Case study

- Further ideas for linking careers with citizenship and PSHE

- Examples of linking the careers curriculum with other areas

- Summary

Linking careers to citizenship and PSHE

Every child matters and their learning is as individual as they are. Learning and development is taking place in the brain as it is bombarded with information all day, every day. To help us to make sense of all the incoming information we construct categories, a type of filing system. The school curriculum runs along the same line with predetermined categories under which information is taught. In most schools the curriculum is still defined by subject areas rather than by different stages in individual development. This is not the most effective way to learn, as pupils' receptivity to different types of learning will depend on their stage of development. If the learning focus is put on individual development, the pupil is put back at the centre of learning.

One way to help break down the barriers and to soften the dividing edges is to plan cross curricular activities. The frameworks for PSHE, citizenship and careers recognise that there are many links between these curriculum areas. Using these links is crucial to allow individual development. If the themes are delivered separately then a young person is bound to become confused, as each area would separately be addressing their self-awareness. The most logical thing to do is to look for the overlap and to plan accordingly.

There are many advantages to linking together careers, PSHE and citizenship.

- It reduces unnecessary repetition.

- Curriculum time for delivery is reduced.

- Each area does not seem to be a 'bolt on' for the pupil.

- Coherence around self-development can be achieved.

- Learning opportunities are maximised.

It is better to do a few things well and in depth than scrape over the surface of many.

Case study

This example is a three-year programme based around self-development in which PSHE, citizenship and careers are integrated. This system has been set up in the school in which I teach and is now being implemented in other schools in the county.

The programme takes place in three stages:

Year 8: take your child to work

Year 9: community service

Year 10: work experience

At each stage self-learning takes place with target-setting for the next stage. Throughout the programme the learning is based upon skills acquisition, development of personal qualities, recognising achievements, the building of a positive self-image and increasing self-esteem. The starting point is to identify the areas from the three frameworks that are applicable.

Year 8 project: take your child to work

This is based on the national scheme 'Take your daughters to work'. Each pupil asks a relative to take them to work on a set day to undertake a work study. The learning outcomes are as follows.

Careers

- Describe how the world of work is changing and identify the skills that promote employability.

- Use the outcomes of self-assessment to identify areas for development, build confidence and develop a positive self-image.

- Use review and reflection to support goal-setting.

Citizenship

- Take part responsibly in community-based activities.

- Reflect on the process of participating.

PSHE

- Relate job opportunities to qualifications and skills.

- Take responsibility.

- Feel positive about themselves.

- Communicate confidently with adults.

There should be a supporting programme in place to maximise the learning potential from the experience. To give focus for pupils they should be set a clear task. For example, during the placement the pupil must find out between three and five interesting facts about work that they did not know before. They can take a photograph of the workplace, ideally using a digital camera, and interview their relative about their work. On returning to school they use the information they have found out to produce a pamphlet using Microsoft Publisher to advertise the workplace. This is then displayed on a year-group display for parents to see at an open evening. In addition each pupil orally presents their pamphlet to their tutor group. Ultimately this is stored in the pupil's Progress File.

The skills used are wide ranging:

- presenting yourself to others

- ICT

- oral and written communication

- carrying out research.

Each pupil completes a self-evaluation questionnaire about their experiences before, during and after the placement. The audit is based upon skills, qualities and achievements where pupils grade themselves on a four-point scale. From this, strengths are identified and celebrated through the use of the Progress File. Two areas for development are identified which, with the help of the tutor, are converted to targets for the year 9 activity. A review of the learning outcomes is also carried out by use of the Progress File.

Year 9 activity: community service

The learning outcomes are as follows (converted into sharp outcomes combining the three frameworks):

- to make a decision based upon research carried out

- to identify two skills and qualities used

- to set a target for work experience

- to use two websites to find out information about the placement

- to be able to identify two examples of voluntary work

- to understand the work of two local community groups

- to be able to identify two areas of success and two areas for development

- to take responsibility.

Each pupil in year 9 undertakes a day's community service. Some placements are based in school, e.g. in the library, in the resources centre or with technicians. Most placements are based in the wider community and the placement hosts include homes for the elderly, luncheon clubs, playgroups, the town council, charity shops, primary schools and the local library.

This forms the main part of the year 9 citizenship project. The pupils, in small groups, are released from a day's timetable in rotation throughout the year. To pull the whole project together each pupil has a community placement passport. This covers the research, first feelings, a supervisor's report, a skills and qualities audit, and pupil self-evaluation with each section.

Pupils carry out research beforehand to establish what service the community group provides and what other provision there is for the client group locally. The research is carried out during a PSHE half-day when placement providers are invited into school to give a workshop about their service. In addition, pupils carry out website searches and use local information leaflets.

After carrying out the research pupils make an informed decision about whether to proceed with the placement or to change client group, which would involve researching an alternative. Before the placement commences pupils have a placement briefing: here their passport is checked, expectations are made clear and the targets set in year 8 are reviewed and altered if necessary. The pupil then knows what they are aiming to achieve personally from the placement.

The supervisor completes a report for the placement day. The day after the placement the pupil takes this to their tutor for a review, during which the pupil is encouraged to discuss whether they had progressed in the area upon which the target was based. This is then projected forward to work experience and anything they would do differently next time. Throughout the programme the pupil is encouraged to be reflective, recognising and celebrating what they did well. They are also given support to develop other areas.

The whole project is tied together in the summer term. The pupil prepares a Powerpoint presentation about their experience and achievements, which is shown to the tutor group. The best presentations for each placement are then shown in an assembly to which the placement providers are invited. The plan for the following year is to show the presentations to parents during a KS4 information evening.

The teacher coordinating the project remarked on how students naturally related their experiences to what they would like to do for work experience. Many pupils were surprised at how rewarded they felt by helping other people, and there was an increase in pupils wanting work-experience placements in caring roles, notably with the elderly.

This particular project works well because it links to prior experiences and self-awareness and links foreward with plans for work experience. The passport brings out the learning aspects of the experience, and through recognising the strengths of each pupil self-esteem is built.

The following quotes from pupils, who were asked to write one sentence about what they found out about themselves by doing the placement, show the value of the experience.

'Before the placement I felt shy and worried about what to say to old people but they were really friendly and I found it quite easy to chat to them.'

'I found out I haven't got the patience to work with small children and it's quite hard work.'

'I was good at serving tea and one man said I make a lovely cuppa so I make tea for my Dad now in the morning.'

'I felt really nervous but I asked some questions and they gave me a good report for communication so I am really pleased with myself.'

'I never thought that I would be good at working with the elderly but the matron said I was a natural and I could come back for work experience, I might like to do it when I leave school now.'

'I liked working in the library because I had to ask people if I could help them. I felt shy at first but then I got more confident and I showed people to where the right books were. I think I improved my communication.'

Year 10 project: work experience

The learning outcomes are as follows.

Careers

- Use self-assessments… to set short-term goals.

- Use work-related learning and direct experience of work to improve their life chances.

- Understand the purpose of interviews.

- Understand what employers are looking for in relation to behaviour at work.

- Review and reflect upon how their experiences have added to their knowledge, understanding and skills.

Citizenship

- Reflect on the process of participating.

PSHE

- Feel positive about themselves.

- Be aware of and assess their personal qualities, skills, achievements and potential to set personal goals.

- Present themselves confidently in a range of situations.

Pupils begin to research work experience options by reviewing their strengths identified in the community placement project. The work experience job families offered to pupils have descriptions about skills and qualities needed so that they can link their strengths to job opportunities.

The aims of work experience will vary according to each pupil's need and prior self-assessments. The key to success is in the linking through target setting from year to year. These are personal self-development targets with the pupil given the support to recognise their strengths at each stage. All this helps to develop self-confidence and self-esteem. Self-reflection becomes second nature to pupils rather than something that is added on as an after thought during year 11. Responsibility for development is placed firmly with the pupil, not something to be done to them by somebody else.

To maximise the learning potential the learning outcomes should be followed through beyond work experience. Skills development should be recognised through other opportunities.

Further ideas for linking careers with citizenship and PSHE

KS3 audit of qualities and skills

This can be developed through school activities and in the wider community. Pupils could write a personal advertisement about themselves for jobs that match their skills and qualities. This could come early in year 9 in preparation for option choices and would be linked to job research. It links to the following elements in the Framework:

- **careers**: 'undertake a realistic self-assessment of their achievements, qualities and aptitudes'

- **PSHE**: 'reflect on and assess their strengths in relation to personality and leisure'

- **citizenship**: 'relate job opportunities to their personal qualifications and skills'

KS3 The changing world of work

After examining changing work patterns pupils could write a story about their work, imagining that they are 50 years in the future. They could produce a time line of all the job changes and work style changes that have happened to them over their imagined working life.

- **careers**: 'describe how the world of work is changing'

- **PSHE**: 'relate job opportunities to the changing world of work'

- **citizenship**: 'relate job opportunities to the changing world of work'

Producing action plans at KS3 for KS4 choices

After an introductory programme based around option choices pupils should use peer support to discuss their choices and the reasons for them. The outcome of this discussion should be a focus for their Individual Learning Plan meeting with tutor and parents. The resulting action plan would become part of the pupil's Progress File.

- **careers**: 'make realistic and informed choices of options available post-14'

- **PSHE**: 'plan realistic targets for KS4'

KS4 Choosing a work experience placement

After recognising their strengths, qualities, aptitudes and skills, pupils make informed choices about their work experience and negotiate their placement accordingly.

- **careers**: 'use review, reflection and action planning to make progress and support career development'

- **PSHE**: 'be aware of and assess their personal qualities, skills, achievement and potential, so that they can set personal goals'

- **citizenship**: 'negotiate, decide and take part responsibly in community based activities'

Examples of linking the careers curriculum with other areas

Work experience preparation

Writing a letter of introduction to their employer could be delivered as part of the year 10 English course.

Work experience

Writing about their experiences can be used as a study for English coursework. The use of ICT in the workplace could be a theme in GCSE ICT coursework.

Activities day

Identifying skills used and qualities shown, reflecting on participation, building a positive self-image are all learning outcomes from PSHE, careers and citizenship.

Summary

Pupils' self-development is at the heart of all their learning. Careers is about developing self-awareness, enabling pupils to make informed decisions about their future. Careers, PSHE and Citizenship combine and complement each other to form the basis of a personal-development curriculum. There are many opportunities for being creative with time and approach of delivery to form a coherent programme with each child at the centre of it.

Chapter 9
LESSON MENUS

- What are three-part lessons?

- Why are three-part lessons effective?

- How to plan three-part careers lessons

- Examples of three-part lessons for careers

- Summary

What are three-part lessons?

An activity that fills a lesson, whether the lesson lasts 30 minutes or an hour, does not engage pupils in learning for that length of time. It has long been accepted that children learn best in blocks of 20 minutes with a change of activity after that time. However, most lessons are not set up to facilitate learning in this way. Breaking up lessons into smaller sections with changes in pace, position in the room and learning style will lead to more effective learning. The change in working should include different groupings, i.e. working individually, paired work, group work or whole-class activities.

A three-part lesson does not always mean three activities. What it does mean is that there should be a starter activity that sets the pace and engages pupils, followed by a main activity (or activities), followed by a plenary activity in which learning is reinforced and evaluated. The separate parts must build upon each other for maximum learning in the classroom. This model is not new and is one of the key principles arising from the National Strategy.

Many colleagues will say that they have been using three-part lessons for years. However, several questions need to be asked:

- Where in the school are three-part lessons being used most effectively?

- What good practice can be shared?

- How can it be shared effectively?

- Are three-part lessons being used by teachers delivering careers lessons?

Experience shows that often even the best practitioners do not transfer their skills when delivering out of their subject area. The aim is to ensure that careers lessons are delivered in the way that ensures accelerated learning. If three-part lessons are not being used consistently by all teachers delivering careers lessons, then you need to consider how to raise awareness and ensure that good practice is implemented and followed.

Why are three-part lessons effective?

Within any group of people there is a range of learning styles. The three key ways are visual learning, auditory learning and kinaesthetic learning. All people learn in all three ways and in some people there is an equal balance. However, in most people one learning style dominates. In any classroom situation you will have spread of pupils learning in different ways, which may mean that they learn in a way that is not compatible with your main teaching style. The three-part lesson can use a range of different strategies to access the three learning styles. This means that there will be a section of the lesson that helps each pupil to learn effectively.

The following quick activity is in the careers curriculum and will help pupils find out their most effective learning style and inform the teacher.

Activity

Prepare three lists of ten simple jobs (i.e. 30 in total). Tell pupils that the aim is that they remember as many of the jobs on each list as they can. Put the first list up on an OHT and give pupils one minute to memorise the jobs. Then cover up the list and ask them to write it out. Total up the score. Read out the second list twice and again ask them to write down what they remember. For the third list ask them to do an action for each job as demonstrated by you, e.g. checking teeth for a dentist. Again ask them to write down the ones that they remember.

Compare the results from the three methods. This is a crude but enjoyable activity that makes the point. You could extend it using all three methods for some more examples; students should find that combining the learning styles makes their memory more effective. You might like to go back and test recall a week later to see if the activity has activated more than the short term memory.

This will raise the teacher's awareness and, when lessons are planned for learning, the different learning styles can be taken into account.

According to Vernon A. Magnesen's 'A Review of Findings from Learning and Memory Retention Studies' (1983): *Innovation Abstracts* 5 (25).

We learn:

10% of what we read

20% of what we hear

30% of what we see

50% of what we see and hear

70% of what we say

90% of what we say and do.

If learning styles are combined, therefore, learning is more effective. By using the three-part lesson model more opportunities are presented for combining reading, hearing, doing and saying. Careers activities such as work experience and enterprise days are powerful opportunities for pupils to learn in the most effective way possible. Magnesen's figures also show that you will not learn effectively by reading a book until you have tried out the ideas in your own classroom.

How to plan three-part careers lessons

There are many careers resources on the market. In most cases learning objectives are followed by an activity that is usually designed to last for an hour. This approach is now outdated because it does not allow learning to be accelerated. When lessons are planned, and careers lessons in particular in this case, the following format should be followed:

- sharp, differentiated learning outcomes displayed throughout the lesson

- a quick-fire starter activity involving the whole class – 10 minutes maximum

- main activity, or series of shorter phased activities depending on lesson length

- plenary activity of 5–10 minutes including revisiting the learning outcomes.

Plan for movement around the room within every lesson. This takes pupils out of comfort zones and the movement activates both sides of the brain.

Once you become used to starter activities it is easy to think of ways to start the lesson. The purpose of starters, and a range of examples, are given in the chapter 'Starters and plenaries' and the ideas can be applied to any context. Thus, if you are doing a lesson on 'Understanding post-16 qualifications' there may not be a starter activity suggested. However, you can take another example and apply the principles, e.g. odd one out, pairing equivalences, true/false statements. Good practice for all staff delivering PSHE or careers is to give a list of starters as part of their toolkit and of course to kick off meetings and training sessions by using starter activities. Teachers themselves also learn more effectively by doing and saying. If you are using a published resource without a starter activity then make sure that the activity is adapted to allow time for a relevant starter to be used.

Main activities have been around for careers education for a long time. When considering whether to use them, or when inventing your own, think about how many learning styles the activity is addressing and whether effective learning will take place. This must be completely tied in with the learning outcomes for the lesson: a published activity may not have been designed to meet the learning outcomes that you are setting out to deliver. If it is a good activity, think whether it could be adapted to fit into a three-part lesson.

Three words that describe good activities that enhance learning are:

- pace

- variety

- challenge.

When you are deciding which activities to use for the main part of your lessons, consider whether they address these three points.

Good activities will also allow for different levels of outcome. The easiest way of doing this is to use 'white space', i.e. by talking to individuals and setting different outcomes by use of instructive words. Identify, describe, explain, hypothesise, formulate, speculate are all hierarchical instructive words which can be used to set different outcomes. These should be prepared in advance and can be easily implemented if pupils are placed either in groups of similar ability or in mixed ability groups with different outcomes for each group member. This will only work with advanced planning, but once groups are established then the organisation becomes far more straightforward.

Main activities must engage all pupils in the learning process. This involves active thought, processing and decision making on an individual level. There should be nobody 'hiding in a corner'. If the level of challenge is right then there should be active participation without the threat of failure. See the example below.

> In class at a primary school each pupil was set the weekly task of selecting an article of news and writing a précis of it. Each child then presented their news article to the rest of the class and it was displayed on the news board. As the Autumn term went on one particular eight-year-old child became more and

> more anxious about completing the news task. At the start of the year she had produced a side of A4, beautifully written, and had pride in her work. By the end of the term the teacher was lucky if she got two short sentences. I asked the child why she no longer liked doing the news. The reason was that, not only did they have to read out their article, they also had to point on a map to any places mentioned in the précis and explain the meaning of any difficult words they had put in.
>
> An activity which certainly presented challenge also presented high threat, the fear of getting things wrong in front of the class and being made to 'feel ridiculous'. The teacher's intentions of getting a high standard of work were thwarted by the threat of the task.

Aim for high challenge, low threat.

Plenary activities are vital to reinforce the learning that has taken place and to reflect upon the lesson. It should also provide opportunity for self-evaluation by the pupils and by the teacher. Plenaries must require an individual response, even if the main activity has been a group task. It is only then that self-reflection can take place.

If learning is to be effective for all pupils then all learning styles must be addressed with the ideas reinforced during the different parts of the lesson. If the learning points have been covered a number of times in a different way then the brain is more likely to retain the information. Alarmingly, research shows that the brain has to process a fact 30 times before it is committed to the long-term memory. This highlights the important nature of reinforcement. All too often we teach something once in just one way and expect pupils to have learnt it. Using links between lessons will also enhance learning because it forces recall and reprocessing.

Examples of three-part lessons for careers

Here are three examples of three-part lessons for careers activities, one taken from each key stage.

KS3: job groupings

Learning outcomes

The learning outcome from the Framework states:

'Use appropriate vocabulary and organise information about work into standard and personally devised groupings.'

This can be converted to sharp learning outcomes to be shared with pupils.

- Know that jobs can be grouped into families (all).

- Be able to construct one job family (most).

- Be able to construct job groups according to personally-devised criteria (some).

Starter activity

Write up on the board 'healthcare'. Ask pupils to write down as many jobs as they can think of in one minute under the job family of healthcare. This should be individual work. Bring the class together and name individuals to give a response. Produce a spider diagram on the board as they feed back ideas.

Main activity

Place pupils in groups of three which are of mixed gender and approximately similar ability (you will need to take a couple of minutes to prepare this before the lesson; if you do not know the class then use data indicators for groupings). Give each group a job family title that they are going to construct. They must produce a spider diagram of the jobs in the family and write a sentence to explain what each one is. Research for this can be carried out using careers leaflets (such as CLIPS leaflets from Lifetime Careers Publishing), websites such as connexionscard.com, files from the careers library and books such as *Occupations*. If you are not able to go to the careers library then you could borrow the folders applicable to the job families that the groups are researching.

Pupils produce a poster such as this:

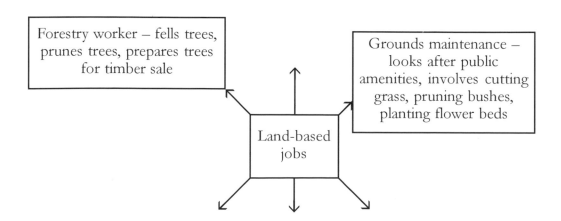

More able pupils should be given a separate task where not only do they research a job family but they also construct groups within it that are based on criteria that they determine, e.g. 'Working with children' could be categorised by age groups of children or by what the work involves such as education, welfare, etc.

Plenary

Each group feeds back for a maximum of one minute on which jobs fall into their job family. Review the learning outcomes with the class: has learning taken place?

KS4: bias in careers information

Learning outcomes

The learning outcome from the Framework states:

'Identify, select and use a wide range of careers information and distinguish between objectivity and bias.' This can be converted into sharp learning outcomes that can be shared with pupils:

- Understand that promotional material might be biased (all).

- Be able to identify three examples of biased information (most).

- Be able to evaluate which sources of information are most reliable (some).

Starter activity

Tape an advertisement from television promoting a career, e.g. the teacher-training agency, the police, the army (if you cannot do this, find a good promotional poster as a stimulus). Show it to the class once and then repeat, asking them to write down two facts about the career and two pieces of publicity information. They will find it hard to find facts and should realise that the information being presented is biased.

Main activity

This works best in small groups constructed according to ability to allow for careful allocation of the jobs. Examples that are less clear cut could go to the more able groups. Make sure all are clear about the difference between objectivity and bias. The group task is to research one job, predetermined according to resources available, looking for biased information and objective information. Good sources to research from are careers reference books, posters, publicity leaflets from professional bodies, careers leaflets, such as CLIPS leaflets published by Lifetime Careers Publishing, websites and prospectuses. Having carried out the research, the pupils write the script for two short television advertisements, one that is biased and one that is objective.

Plenary

Present the advertisements as sound bites. Review the learning outcomes with the class: has learning taken place?

An extension to this, for example as part of a PSHE day or in conjunction with performing arts, is for the class to act out and video the best two advertisements. They could even compose music to accompany it.

Post-16: personal influences

Learning outcomes

The learning outcome from the Framework states:

'Evaluate the impact of external influences on personal views, attitudes, behaviour and careers plans and respond appropriately.' This can be converted to sharp learning outcomes.

- Identify 3-5 people who influence your decision making.

- For each one, identify at least one relevant personal value.

- Evaluate how their personal values compare to your own.

Starter activity

Give an account of your own career path (or a fictional one) stressing key decision points and who has influenced you when making those decisions. Students then brainstorm types of people who have an influence on their decision making, e.g. parents, friends, tutor, personal/careers adviser, work experience contacts, etc.

Main activity

Individually pupils construct their own mind map of all the people who have influenced their decision making in the past and who currently influence their decision making. In order to work, this activity must be intensely personal to the pupil and it may throw up some difficult issues such as pressures put on them by parents or partners. On the map they should write down the relevant values held by these people. They should then add their own values. The difficult part is for students to take a step back and analyse whether they have their own opinion and values about their future or whether they are mirroring what others wish them to do. Sometimes conflict will arise where pupils are opposing their parents' opinions and values. This may be a genuine conflict, arising from their own belief and value system, or it may be based upon a knee-jerk reaction. Either way, delicate and difficult discussions may arise.

Plenary

Each student feeds back one thing that they have realised by undertaking this activity, but they must have the right to pass.

Summary

Plan three-part lessons for careers to accelerate learning within the classroom. This leads to greater engagement by pupils and allows a wider range of learning styles to be accessed. It allows for repetition in ideas, which reinforces the learning points.

Chapter 10
SHARP OUTCOMES

- What are sharp outcomes?

- Using learning outcomes to accelerate learning

- How to convert learning objectives into sharp outcomes

- Case study: lesson observations focusing on the use of learning outcomes

- Summary

What are sharp outcomes?

There was once a fish seller who had a stall at the market. On a board at the side of the stall he had written: 'Lovely, fresh, wet fish for sale today'. A lady stopped to read the sign. Others, however, were passing by quickly as it was beginning to rain. After a few moments the lady approached the stall keeper.

'Sir, please may I make a suggestion that would attract more people to your stall?' she started.

Business had been slow that day and, eager to hear a way to improve his sales, he leant forward. 'Well, what is it?' he replied.

'You have too many words on your sign. Nobody is going to stop and read it in this weather.'

The fish seller came round to the front of the stall and stood alongside her looking at the sign. Reluctantly, he agreed that she was right. 'But how do I make it better?' he asked.

'You tell me,' the lady said.

'Well, of course I am selling something, I am a market stall.'

The lady took a pen and crossed out 'for sale'.

'And of course it is today,' and so this too was crossed out.

'All fish are wet, I suppose and of course my fish are fresh, I wouldn't say anything else. Come to that they are lovely too'.

Together they looked at the sign, which now just read: 'fish'.

It has been recognised for some time that it is important to share learning outcomes with pupils so that they have a focus for the lesson. What has been less well documented is how to make the learning outcomes as sharp as possible in order to accelerate learning within the classroom. It is easy to fall into the trap of the stall keeper and share something with pupils that is wordy and vague, and which is detrimental rather than advantageous to learning. Recent research has shown that boys in particular learn best with a clear focus to the lesson. If they are given sharp learning outcomes with differentiation, they are motivated by the challenge of aiming for the more advanced outcome. In addition, all students will know that learning is expected rather than merely having a series of tasks to complete. The two are very different: pupils may complete a series of tasks without engaging thought processes, and then very limited or no learning may be taking place.

Golden rules for learning outcomes are as follows.

- Give three or less, never more.

- Keep them short.

- Differentiate the outcomes to address learning for all members of the class.

- Model language which you want pupils to use.

- Write them up somewhere so that you and pupils can refer back to them.

Using learning outcomes to accelerate learning

The learning outcomes need to be in place before a lesson is planned. Pupil learning must be at the heart of everything that you do in the classroom. With all lessons plan what you want the pupils to learn, not what you want them to do. Teachers delivering careers will be working out of their first subject area. Sometimes an activity is photocopied and given to pupils with little thought as to what they will learn through completing the activity. If the teacher is not clear about the outcomes, then the pupils will be even less clear. Only when the outcomes are in place can lesson activities be put together that will facilitate learning. This is much easier to do if a three-part lesson is planned, with a starter to set the pace and focus, then the main learning activity followed by a plenary in which learning is assessed. The whole lesson becomes much sharper because success can be monitored within the lesson by the teacher and by the pupils.

Learning outcomes are different to learning objectives. Learning objectives are what the teacher will deliver to the whole class. Learning outcomes are what each pupil should learn during the lesson, which in an ideal world would be individual to the pupil, taking into account ability, prior learning and emotional ability. This is not an ideal world and 30 different learning outcomes cannot be planned for, but planning three levels of outcome is a realistic target. Again, to work effectively the teacher must know the class well to allow mental mapping for groups of pupils. Learning is at its best when the teacher is so emotionally aware that during the lesson they are directing students to their individual outcomes by dialogue, using leaders such as 'From you I am looking for…', 'What would happen if…?' Learning is less effective if the careers teacher has no relationship with the class and is teaching on a carousel basis. It is better to have an atmosphere of shared trust, so a teacher who is a tutor of the group, with minimal coaching and support, is probably better placed to deliver careers education. In best practice a careers lesson would not even be identified as such, because the learning outcomes would be integrated with other subject areas, usually, as suggested in the chapter 'Joined-up thinking', PSHE and citizenship.

How to convert learning objectives into sharp outcomes

Learning objectives for each key stage are published in *Careers Education and Guidance – a National Framework 11–19*. There are so many links with citizenship and PSHE that a mapping process integrating the three should occur before launching into delivering the learning objectives for careers.

The learning objectives are too cumbersome for pupils and are not sharp, so the first stage is to convert one into sharp learning outcomes. For example, a learning objective taken from KS3 concerning self-development reads:

'Recognise stereotyped and misrepresented images of people, careers and work and how their own views of these issues affect their decision making'.

This learning objective may need to be addressed in two stages and could form lessons in year 7 and again in year 9 in preparation for decision making around option choices. It would be effective if linked to a drama or English topic. In year 7 learning outcomes from this objective might be as follows.

- All should identify three stereotyped images of people.

- Most should be able to explain what a stereotype is.

- Some should be able to construct a stereotypical view of one area of work.

In Year 9 learning outcomes from this objective might be as follows.

- All should be able to describe three examples of stereotyped jobs.

- Most should be able to determine three stereotypical work roles from case studies.

- Some will be able to construct two possible career paths, one following their stereotypical view and one going against it.

From this three points emerge. First, by using the 'all, most, some' model for framing outcomes there is immediate differentiation. Secondly, the instructive words are progressive in complexity – identify, explain and construct – which again brings about differentiation. Thirdly, if numbers are put in then the outcomes

are sharpened and success can be measured. In this example, rather than 'Describe stereotypical work roles' a number has been introduced: 'Determine three stereotypical work roles.' With the first outcome a pupil or the teacher does not know if one example means success or whether ten examples are needed, whereas success can be clearly identified with the second example.

Once the outcomes are in place then the activities naturally follow on. The year 7 lesson may open with a starter that flashes up seven images of people: pupils are asked to write down what they think each person does for a job (this works best if the lesson is not introduced as one about stereotype, so that pupils are caught unaware and give instinctive answers). A brief discussion would follow about what a stereotype is. Next comes a group activity with pupils placed in predetermined groups according to ability with a mix of boys and girls. In their groups they would be given images of people at work. The task is to divide them into stereotyped images and non-stereotyped images. Give ambiguous and thought-provoking images to the more able groups. Each group would feedback with one example that they want to share. Again, encourage more able groups to feed back with a challenging one. For the plenary the teacher could model a job that is stereotyped, e.g. 'All mechanics are young, white males with spots and oily overalls'. Give pupils five minutes to come up with their own example; give out prompt cards to anyone who is struggling after the first minute. Ask pupils to read out their ideas. Remember that you are not expecting all pupils to be able to do this unaided; this is the 'some' part of the lesson.

The year 9 lesson would build upon prior learning and allow for a greater level of emotional intelligence in pupils. In year 9 the issue of stereotypes must be related to the influences around them and how they see themselves in society. If the learning objectives are interpreted in this way then immediately there is progression and you avoid comments such as: 'We've done stereotypes before.'

Example year 9 lesson

This lesson might begin with a brainstorm of all the people who have influences upon them, e.g. parents, teachers, friends, neighbours, TV role models, etc. It is effective if the teacher models the purpose of the lesson by mapping key influences in their own life and by describing how each has affected their decision making. Pupils then pair up with a critical friend and have a minute each to describe someone in their life who influences their decision making and what values that person stands for. Individually pupils produce a mind map of all the people who influence them, what jobs they do, what values they stand for. If done properly this is a powerful exercise because most pupils find that their career ideas are based upon fulfilling their own self-image of where they stand in society. Pupils then do two imaginary career paths for themselves, one going with the stereotypical image that they have created of themselves and the other going for something completely different that they never would have thought of before. The plenary would be a sharing of what each pupil has found out about themselves. The following lesson or tutor period would link what they have found out to how their new awareness might influence their decision making for option choices.

It is important to review the learning outcomes with the pupils. This should take place either within each section of the lesson, which helps with motivation particularly with less able groups, or at the end to allow self-evaluation by the pupils and by the teacher. It is important to have the learning outcomes displayed in the room so that these progress checks can be made. If the expected level of learning has not taken place then it means that the lesson has not been effective. The model of delivery needs to be flexible enough that opportunity is given to revisit the learning outcomes, but with different activities to reinforce the learning. If delivered by tutors, there is often a registration period that could be constructively used to follow up.

The main feature from these examples is that if the learning is planned for, then the activities will naturally follow on and everybody knows what is expected of them and can measure their success. There is progression in the level of emotional intelligence required to cope with the issues. This enhances learning.

Case study: lesson observations focusing on the use of learning outcomes

I carried out a series of observations of year 10 lessons at a school. The careers lessons were taught by specialist careers teachers who were members of a PSHE team. They were taught in six-week blocks to mixed-ability tutor groups in a carousel arrangement as part of a PSHE programme. I was particularly focusing on the use of learning outcomes and how they affected the degree of learning that took place.

The lesson observations are from two experienced, established teachers. I was told that the lesson was part of a sequence of debriefing activities following a week's work experience that took place in May. It was now two months later because these groups had been doing other PSHE activities as part of the rotation. The teacher with responsibility for careers had planned the lesson and had given a lesson plan to the other teacher to deliver later in the week. I asked which learning objective the lesson was based upon and was shown, from the Framework: 'review and reflect on how their experiences have added to their knowledge, understanding and skills.'

Lesson one – delivered by the teacher with responsibility for careers

The class were late coming in from PE saying that they had been down at the swimming pool. The pupils came in over a seven-minute period and automatically sat down and began to chat to each other. There was debate with the teacher about who was away and who they were waiting for; then a register was taken in silence, now nearly ten minutes into the lesson.

The pupils were told that the purpose of the lesson was to 'think about work experience and to find out what skills and qualities you have got through doing it'. The aim was then written on the board – 'to find out about what you learnt from doing work experience' – and pupils were asked to write this down in their folders. The teacher then instructed pupils to draw a table in their book with two columns headed 'My skills on work experience' and 'My qualities on work experience'. They were told they had 15 minutes to write a list for each. One pupil asked what the difference between them was and the teacher replied that a quality was something that you had and a skill was something that you learnt. The pupils worked in silence for ten minutes whilst the teacher guided two less able pupils at the back of the class.

After this time, talk started to break out as pupils compared with each other what they had written. One girl put her hand up and asked whether what she had written was correct. Under the skills section she had written, 'I had a card and £10 at the end of the week'. When the teacher read this out to the class the pupils dissolved into laughter. The pupils were asked to put their work into their folders. The teacher then gave out a worksheet entitled 'Skills for work experience', which was a list of skills. Pupils were again given 15 minutes to circle any skills that they used and to add to the list.

The final task was to write a paragraph for their folder about what they did on work experience, incorporating the skills that they had used. During this time the teacher circulated and gave help to pupils who were struggling by suggesting how they make a start. Pupils ran out of time for this and most were left unfinished.

The class were dismissed.

In the afternoon registration period I gave a simple questionnaire to pupils and to the teacher to assess whether learning had taken place. I divided these into gender groups to see if this had any bearing upon the results.

The number of respondents were 13 girls, 15 boys and the teacher. For the teacher the text was adapted, i.e. for statement 1 it read, 'I understood what pupils were supposed to learn during the lesson'.

Results from the questionnaire

The pupils circled a number for each statement where

1 = strongly agree	3 = disagree
2 = agree	4 = strongly disagree

Statement	Total responses			
	1	**2**	**3**	**4**
I understood what I was supposed to learn during the lesson — Boys	0	2	8	5
Girls	1	3	7	2
Teacher	1			
The activities during the lesson helped me to learn — Boys	0	0	7	8
Girls	0	4	6	3
Teacher		1		
The teacher helped me to understand what I was expected to achieve — Boys	0	2	5	8
Girls	1	4	3	5
Teacher		1		
In my opinion I learnt well during this lesson — Boys	0	2	8	5
Girls	0	5	5	3
Teacher			1	
In my opinion I completed the activities to the best of my ability — Boys	0	0	10	5
Girls	2	4	3	4
Teacher		1		
I enjoyed this lesson — Boys	1	2	5	7
Girls	3	5	4	1
Teacher		1		

Conclusions

Although the aims of the lesson were shared with the class the learning outcomes were not made explicit, nor were they differentiated. The opening task was valid. However, it was not set within a context and the explanation of 'a skill' and 'a quality' was not clear. No examples were given and pupil understanding was not checked either before or during the task. The skills audit was completed by most students with some success although the purpose and outcome of this activity was not clear. The final piece of open writing suited the most able students but the majority of the class would have benefited from a writing frame. Insufficient time was allowed.

There was little evidence of the pupils' work being checked and there were no opportunities for them to receive feedback. As a result of the lesson pupils did not seem to have a better understanding of what they had achieved by undertaking work experience, nor an awareness of how this might have a bearing on future opportunities. There was no summing up at the end of the lesson.

From the pupil questionnaire it is apparent that boys rated the lesson lower than the girls. Overall 21% of pupils understood what was expected of them from the lesson. This leaves 79% of pupils starting the lesson from a confused standpoint. This does not set up a climate for learning. Ratings are not high in any of the areas questioned and limited learning has taken place. This would place this lesson as unsatisfactory on an Ofsted rating. The teacher's perception of his own performance is higher than the pupil feedback would suggest.

This lesson is fairly typical of careers lessons where the teacher does not know the pupils well. The teacher has planned activities to fill the lesson and pupils have completed most of them and for the majority of the time have been on task. Because of this the teacher thought that this had been a successful lesson. He did, upon reflection, realise that he had not planned what learning should take place by doing the activities that he had put together.

Lesson two – delivered by the colleague

Before the class entered the room the teacher had written on the board: 'Write down three skills that you used on work experience.' The pupils came into the room, got out their equipment, looked at the board and started writing. When all the pupils had entered the room and had begun the task the teacher asked the pupils to come and sit in a circle in the centre of the room bringing with them what they had written. The pupils did this quickly and quietly. The teacher turned on the overhead projector upon which there were three learning outcomes written.

- Describe the difference between a skill and a quality.

- Give examples of three skills and three qualities that you used on work experience.

- Suggest how you could use a skill and a quality again in a different context.

She went through these with the class, making it explicit that by the end of the lesson all should be able to explain the difference, most will give three examples of skills and qualities, and some pupils would be able to say how they could use their skills and qualities in a new way.

She then went on to describe a skill as something that you 'can do' and gave some examples. She went round the circle with each student giving one skill that they had used. The teacher then described a quality as something that you are, and again gave examples. The pupils were given one minute to think of a quality that they demonstrated on work experience and again suggestions went round the circle, with any misconceptions being challenged.

The pupils were then paired up by topping and tailing the register and asked to sit opposite each other. The teacher explained that one person was to be the interviewer and the other person the interviewee about their work experience. Then they were to swap over. They had four minutes in which to conduct each interview. Numbered questions were placed on the OHT which followed a sequence, starting with 'Where did you go on work experience?', and then asking what tasks they did, what skills they used with examples, etc. The pupils were all on task and the teacher circulated, unobtrusively pulling up a chair to listen in on conversations. After the interview each pair was asked to give one thing that their partner had achieved from work experience. The teacher used two examples to explain how the skills that they had used could be used in different situations and she introduced the words 'transferable skill'.

In the final activity students were given a writing frame to complete individually. This was split into five short sections and summarised the outcomes from the lesson. This included their top three skills and qualities with one line of evidence and skills that they could use in new situations.

A few minutes before the end of the lesson the teacher put back the OHT with the learning outcomes. As she read out each one she asked the pupils to raise their hands if they felt they had achieved each outcome. Without counting exactly, I gained the impression that the responses were overwhelmingly positive. The teacher collected in the writing-frame sheets, congratulated everyone on a good lesson and dismissed the class.

Again in the afternoon registration time I gave the class the same questionnaire as I had used with the previous group. The number of respondents were 16 girls, 14 boys and the teacher.

Results from the questionnaire

Statement	Total responses				
		1	**2**	**3**	**4**
I understood what I was supposed to learn during the lesson	Boys	6	8	0	0
	Girls	10	5	1	0
	Teacher	1			
The activities during the lesson helped me to learn	Boys	10	3	1	0
	Girls	12	4	0	0
	Teacher		1		
The teacher helped me to understand what I was expected to achieve	Boys	0	10	4	0
	Girls	7	6	2	0
	Teacher		1		
In my opinion I learnt well during this lesson	Boys	9	3	1	0
	Girls	8	5	3	0
	Teacher	1			
In my opinion I completed the activities to the best of my ability	Boys	12	2	0	0
	Girls	10	3	3	0
	Teacher		1		
I enjoyed this lesson	Boys	6	4	4	0
	Girls	8	5	2	1
	Teacher		1		

Conclusions

There was a relevant starter activity that engaged the pupils in the lesson as soon as they entered the classroom. The learning outcomes were clear and differentiated and shared with the pupils. The activities in the lesson had pace, variety and challenge, and all pupils participated throughout. The activities drew upon each pupil's direct experiences and therefore all responded well to the activities. The subject-specific language was correctly used with examples given to illustrate their meaning, and pupils' understanding was checked. The final written activity pulled together the discussion points that had been previously made and this work was collected in by the teacher to enable feedback to be given. Success was measured within the lesson by revisiting the learning outcomes at the end, with individual responses required.

Pupil responses from the questionnaire were positive, with no discernable gender differential. The teacher was aware of what learning she expected to take place and was able to evaluate this accurately. Of the class 97% were aware of what learning was expected from the start of the lesson, with 87% saying they had learnt well during the lesson. This lesson would have been judged very good using Ofsted criteria.

Comparisons and overall conclusions

The teacher delivering the first lesson had planned what activities were to take place during the hour and had learning objectives in place. The learning, however, was limited by the teacher's lack of awareness about what he wanted pupils to achieve. The girls assessed their learning as higher than the boys did. This could reflect the current research that boys need very tight structure with clear learning outcomes to learn effectively. Alternatively, the boys in this class may have assessed themselves more harshly than the girls.

The second teacher had converted these objectives into learning outcomes with different learning expectations for different groups of pupils. As a result, the second teacher had thought through how to deliver the lesson to ensure that effective learning was taking place. By checking the pupils' evaluation at the end of the lesson the teacher could also judge whether the lesson had been successful. The content engaged and motivated both boys and girls and all were eager to participate. The results were borne out by the questionnaire with accelerated learning having taken place.

Far more research would need to be done to assess whether it was the sharp learning outcomes, teaching skills, difference in pupils or, more probably, a combination of all three that accelerated the learning in the second example. Nevertheless, this methodology can be used with any class to enable a teacher to evaluate a lesson, or a sequence of lessons.

As a result of the research carried out in this case study the first teacher asked to plan a lesson jointly with his colleague, identifying the learning outcomes as a starting point. Peer observation was carried out when the lesson was delivered with a similar follow-up questionnaire completed by pupils. The results from both classes were more positive than previously.

Summary

Sharp outcomes are essential to any lesson that is of a good standard or better. The lesson is framed in a context that enables both boys and girls to access learning more effectively. In careers lessons sharp outcomes can considerably raise the expectations of the teacher and the pupils. If lessons are delivered by a number of teachers for whom careers is not their first subject, it can lead to a dramatic raising of standards and to greater consistency between groups. Only with sharp outcomes can true self-evaluation and continued professional development take place.

Chapter 11
STARTERS AND PLENARIES

- What are starter activities?

- Examples of starters

- Starters for careers

- What are plenaries?

- Activities for plenaries in careers

- Summary

What are starter activities?

Starter activities are an essential component of each lesson. They set the pace and tone in order to engage, motivate and stimulate thought. A starter should be fun, take no more than ten minutes to complete, and set the context of the lesson. The activity should be linked with the learning outcomes and can be used to gauge prior understanding. Aim for high challenge and low threat. Once the class routines become established, pupils will anticipate a starter activity and will come in eager to begin thinking and learning.

Starters have high impact on learners for minimal teacher effort. They act as a stimulus and trigger a conditioned response for learning. Before you begin, explain to pupils why you are using starter activities – to warm up their brain to help them to learn more effectively. Some classes find starters easier to accept if the teacher goes into some of the theory about different learning styles and stimulating both sides of the brain to help to lay down nervous pathways for memory. It also helps if the pupils have to move to take part in the activity. The extra oxygen supply gives a boost to the brain and helps to focus the mind. Do not expect immediate success when introducing starter activities; it takes time to establish good practice. It may be tempting to give up if your first attempt is stressful and unsuccessful. However, be self-evaluative and, if necessary, ask a critical friend to observe you and make suggestions on how to improve.

Examples of starters

There are two types of starter. The first is for individuals to begin work as soon as they step into the classroom. It is effective if pupils are coming to the lesson over a staggered period, e.g. from a PE lesson. It avoids the dead learning time between the arrival of the first and the last pupils during which pupils are chatting and lose their readiness to learn. As the pupils come in they are given their first task, which could be written on the board, handed to them on a card, displayed on an interactive white board or on an OHT. Large eye-catching photographs work well. The task should require thought and an individual response so that all pupils are immediately engaged. It acts as a 'warm up' for the learning that is going to take place. The brain becomes engaged in thinking processes so the right connections are being made. Good openers that can be attached to any learning outcomes include:

write down three examples of...

write out these five examples in order of priority

pick out five key words from this paragraph of text

write down three things that you learnt last lesson

what three things do you think of when you see this photograph?

Giving a target number of responses required makes the teacher expectation clear. It also allows the last pupil entering the room the opportunity to come up with something, which means positive participation. Threes or fives are the most effective, although you can add challenge by using phrases such as 'as many as you can think of in three minutes', with a predetermined privilege for the winner. Set a short time limit, usually one minute after the last person joins the group. At the end of this time bring the class together to share responses.

The second type of starter is for a class entering the room together. This must engage pupils collectively. Before you begin, move the pupils so that they are out of their places. Ask them to stand in a circle or a line, or to sit around the front. This takes the pupils away from their territory and shows group bonding. These starters will have a different feel and a key feature for success is to engage everyone in the activity. The following strategies work well.

- Use a hands-down policy for a **question and answer session**. Make it explicit to pupils that they all have to think of an answer and that they have seven seconds to think of it (this time is in line with current educational guidance, allowing thought processes to formulate a response to an open question). Choose who will answer, which provides an opportunity for differentiation. Start with descriptive questions and recall, progressing to explanations and opinions, and then to speculative questioning: 'What if . . . ?' This allows for appropriate challenge.

- Use **wipe boards** for quick-fire responses to questions.

- Use a **true/false quiz** with ten prepared questions: use wipe boards with T on one side and F on the other so pupils can flash responses. Or give out red and green cards: these can be used to establish opinions (agree/disagree), or to establish a starting point for the level of understanding in the group.

- **Loop cards** with a question on one side and an answer to a different question on the other side. Give an opening question and the class look at the answer side of the card. If they have the answer then they ask the next question. A health warning with this is that pupils are slow to begin with, so the activity can reduce pace rather than step it up. You could have two teams set against each other to speed things up.

- Use **brain gym** to get both sides of the brain actively involved. The theory is that this accelerates learning. There are many examples, but a simple one is to use arm movement at the same time as chanting a sequence of words. Put L (left arm up), R (right arm up) or B (both arms up) under the words. Chant with arm movements and repeat several times until a smooth rhythm is set up. You will know this one works when children pass you in the corridor and start chanting and swinging their arms about.

- **Odd one out:** give three words and ask the pupils to decide which is the odd one out. There are no wrong answers to this one but the pupil must be able to explain their choice.

- **Hot seating:** choose one pupil to be the expert and the rest of the class think up one question each to ask.

- **Kim's game:** place an image on an OHT and cover it. Flash the image and ask the pupils to draw what they see. Repeat again and again until a more accurate image is built up.

- Show a **photograph** and ask the pupils to make seven observations about it.

- Use interactive **PowerPoint activities**.

Starters for careers

Careers lessons can be used as a tool to model good practice. The following are the top twenty starter activities based on the CEG framework.

The skills and qualities chant

This can be used before a self-assessment skills and qualities audit with year 9 students or year 10 to highlight differences between skills and qualities. Prepare an OHT with randomly distributed skills and qualities words. Ask students to chant the words, raising their right arm for a quality and their left arm for a skill. Keep repeating until the class is synchronised in their arm raising, and the pace is smooth and fast. This is a fun way to learn the vocabulary needed for self-awareness audits.

Photographs and stereotypes

This activity can be used with all age groups as an introduction to 'What is stereotyping?', 'Challenging stereotypes' or discrimination. Prepare seven photographs of adults of different ages, races and gender on an OHT, PowerPoint or large laminated cards. Don't have them in a work environment. Give pupils five seconds to look at each and write down the job that they think the person does. This works better if the word stereotype is not mentioned before the activity. It raises useful discussion points about judging people on their looks, about what is a stereotype, and about whether the pupils have shown prejudice. This activity could be adapted for a lesson on discrimination if pupils are asked to choose one person for a fictional job, e.g. a doctor.

Goal setting and aspirations

'Dear diary'

This activity could be used in year 9 when introducing individual goal-setting. It involves reading a piece, such as the following, written by a teenager about herself.

All about me

Dear Diary

Well, what about me? Last night I lay awake in bed listening to my mum and step-dad, Dave, arguing. It was about my little sister, she's 13 and stayed out late. Because she's the youngest they don't give her the grief they give me. My mum says she should be grounded but Dave says she's got to be allowed to go out. I can't wait to get out of here and away from them all, to get away from all of the arguments. I wish my mum would see that I'm not all bad, she's always on at me: 'tidy up your room', 'look after your sister', 'cook the tea', 'go

---

and get some milk from the garage'. She never says thank you and she complains that she has to do all the work around here.

One day I will be away from it all. I might miss them ...but there again. I want to be a policewoman, you see, not just a PC but one of those detectives like you see on the TV. I know I can do it if I try hard. I want a big house, maybe in a village or a nice town, not one like this where people graffiti and throw rubbish in the river. I want a husband and kids, a family where we don't always argue. My mum says going to university is a waste of time and I need to get a job next year, earn some money. I don't want to do that. I want to go to university, maybe to do psychology so I can find out about people's minds to help me to be a great detective. My teachers say I can do it. I need to get Bs in my GCSEs and I can do it, I know I can. Then A levels next, I really want to do biology. My mum says I spend too much time shut in my bedroom listening to music, she doesn't know what I'm really doing. I hide my books when she comes in, you see, put a magazine on top of them so she doesn't make fun of me. 'Head stuck in a book again, waste of time they are, just like you.'

I want to travel, not just stay in a hotel, but really travel and see how other people live. I'm saving up my money from my job at Sainsbury's, but mum doesn't know that either. I fancy India first, somewhere hot and exciting. Then maybe Australia, I'd love to trek in the outback.

Explain the difference between a goal and an aspiration. Give each pupil a wipe board and allocate them to pick out either three goals or three aspirations. Ask them to listen to the reading the first time without writing anything down, then to listen again writing down the three examples. Feed back the examples they have found.

Recognising achievements by modelling

This can be used for any age group where pupils are going to write about their achievements and the skills and qualities that they demonstrate. The teacher needs to think this through beforehand. They should describe to the class an achievement in their life. The pupils suggest which skills and qualities are demonstrated in the example. They could do this by 'hands down' responses or by using wipe boards.

Health and safety in the workplace

This is the Kim's game idea, used for work experience preparation with years 10 or 11. Cover an OHT of a workplace showing health and safety hazards. Show the image for 30 seconds and ask pupils to look and find the hazards. Cover the image and give one minute for them to write them down.

What's my line?

This is a good general warm up for careers lessons and can be used to break up lessons or in ten-minute tutorial slots. It is useful before doing research into different jobs. Think of a job (you may need to find some information on it beforehand, from 'Explorer' or a job book). The pupils are allowed 20 questions to find out what you do. They are not allowed to ask 'Are you a …?' but have to ask information-seeking questions that you can only answer 'yes' or 'no' to, e.g. 'Do you work out of doors?' At the end of the 20 questions they can guess what you do.

Labour market information

Useful for KS4 and sixth form, use this to kick off a lesson on labour market trends. Prepare a list of 10 jobs that are either growing or declining. Pupils can give their response in a number of ways, e.g. using wipe boards with G and D on, or two colours of flash cards.

Spot the odd one out – for job groups

This can be used before careers research in KS3 to get across the idea of researching families of jobs as career areas, rather than looking for one specific job. Give related jobs and one non-related, e.g. physiotherapist, occupational therapist, speech therapist, physicist. Repeat for different groups.

Catch game – for grouping jobs

This is useful for KS3 where job groupings are being investigated. The learning objective is to see links between jobs. It works best if pupils stand in a circle. Give a job group, e.g. working in care, and throw a ball to one person. They have to say a care job and throw the ball to someone else, who says a different job, etc. Aim for ten jobs in each category. After ten give the second category, e.g. working outdoors.

Guess that job – loop cards

A good warm-up for any lesson about work roles and skills. Each card contains information about a job on one side, e.g. 'I work for clients', 'I produce design drawings', 'I need a good eye for colour', 'I need to be good at working to scale', 'I make the inside of houses look better'. On the opposite side there would be an unrelated job title. On the back of another card would be 'I am an interior designer'. This pupil then reads out their job description ... and so it goes on.

Charades – for qualities or skills

This can be split up over several lessons or short tutorial periods. Put the class in two teams. Give each pupil a separate card with a word on it which they have one minute to act out to the rest of the team, who have to guess what it is. Keep a score sheet and get the competition going. This is good for tutor group bonding.

Pictionary

This is the same idea as above but it can be applied to a wide range of subjects, e.g. changing employment trends. You could give titles of jobs that are either current, e.g. graphic designer, or were current 100 years ago, e.g. butler. The pupil has one minute to draw the job whilst the team guesses what it is.

Job associations

Put up a title of an industry which involves many job roles, e.g. 'the fashion industry', 'the media' or 'the travel industry'. Pair up pupils and give them three minutes to write down as many jobs as they can associated with the industry. This is useful to broaden pupils' awareness of the diversity of jobs associated with industries. It can be used as a preparation for work experience to avoid pupils saying things such as 'I want to work in the media.'

Looking for links in job families

Write up five jobs that belong to the same job family, e.g. nursing auxiliary, nurse, care assistant, doctor, consultant. Ask pupils to write down three to five things that they have in common. This is to get across the idea that the same skills, qualities and work environment are involved but different qualification levels and training are needed.

Identifying skills

Explain what a skill is. Ask pupils to write down three to five skills that they have used today, e.g. getting to school on time, meeting a deadline, etc. Use this as an introduction to skills.

CVs

Put up an OHT or slide of an extract from a CV. Ask pupils to read it on their own and to pick out good points and weak points. Ask for volunteers to come up and point out what they have picked out.

Goal-setting

Read out extracts from an autobiography of a famous person and give pupils clues to work out which person it is about.

Identifying sources of help for options in year 9

Ask pupils to think shower any person from whom they could get guidance and advice, and then do the same for sources of information.

Managing change and transition

Read out two personal accounts of people who have made a transition, one that was successful and one that was less successful. Pupils discuss what factors determine whether a transition was successful or not.

Reviewing transitions

Ask pupils to give themselves a score on a scale of one to ten indicating how successful they were at making their last transition. This opens up discussion leading to transition review and can be used at any key stage.

What are plenaries?

A plenary takes place at the end of a lesson, usually during the last five to ten minutes. It is an activity which involves the whole class and reviews the learning that has taken place within the lesson. They are used for four main reasons:

- for pupils to use the new knowledge or concept taught in the lesson to reinforce the learning

- for pupils to assess whether they have met the learning outcomes for the lesson, therefore showing that progress has been made

- as a tool of self-evaluation for the teacher to gauge the success of the lesson

- to have an active and strong end of the lesson, therefore maximising the time for learning.

The same rules apply for plenaries as for starter activities. All pupils should be actively involved; the activity should relate to the learning that has taken place; the plenary should be fun and engaging; and there should be evidence that learning has taken place.

Activities for plenaries in careers

In the following ideas for plenaries, the methodologies can be used in many situations.

True or false

Give pupils an individual wipe board with T on one side and F on the other. Give ten true-or-false questions related to the learning in the lesson. The same idea can be used with S and Q for skill and quality, with pupils indicating which is which from a list.

Jobs and skills

Give pupils individual cards with a skill on. Put two sheets of sugar paper on the floor with a job title on each. Stand the pupils round in a circle, give them seven seconds' thinking time and then ask them to place the card on the paper relating to the job that the skill would be needed for. Give skills which could go in either to more able pupils. Ask for justifications of the placing.

Wonderwall

Put up ten answers to questions on an OHT which are arranged randomly and then numbered 1-10. Put pupils in pairs and give each pair a wipe board and pen. Read out a question and give ten seconds for pupils to decide which answer goes with the question and to write the number down. Give a countdown of three and ask the numbers to be displayed.

Ask the experts

This can be done with most topics. An example would be for labour market information. Three people offer to form a panel of experts. The rest of the class, in pairs or individually, write down a relevant question about the topic to ask the expert panel. The panel then asks for the questions from the class and take it in turns to answer. If they are unable to answer, they can consult the teacher before giving their reply.

Priorities

This is done individually. Pupils put three statements in rank order. The questions can be prepared in advance or pupils can make up their own. If the theme were 'People who influence their decision making', pupils would write down three people who influence them in impact order. Give them one minute to do this. Give two minutes to explain to a partner who influences them and why, and then swap over.

Show and tell

This is where the lesson activities result in something visible which can be shown to the rest of the class. For example a poster, diagram or role play can be displayed, with some individuals explaining their thought processes behind it. In a lesson on goals, aspirations and barriers pupils may complete their own 'Where am I heading?' diagram. Put pupils in a group of three where they are given two minutes to decide which one to show and tell. The groups hold up a diagram and describe what they have put and why.

Continuum lines

This can be done in any situation where pupils will have an opinion about an issue, e.g. whether they value unpaid work. This can be done physically by using the walls as a scale and asking pupils to place themselves at the appropriate place in the room. If this is too disruptive, an alternative is to give a score out of ten, ten being that they highly value it, and feed back their scores to gauge opinion in a class.

What have you found out?

When pupils have been carrying out research, e.g. using ICT to match skills to occupations, they feed back one fact that they have found out.

What next?

This idea is similar to the one above but can be applied to any form of action planning where individual follow-up is needed. Pupils state one piece of action they are going to take within the next week. In the following lesson this can provide the starter to see who has done what they said. If you want to be particularly nasty, you can video their pledges as a reminder.

Traffic lights

This can be used to check pupil understanding. Each pupil is given a set of red, amber and green flash cards. The teacher reads out a set of ten statements based on the learning outcomes of the lesson. The pupil holds up the appropriate coloured card in response.

red: I don't get it

amber: I'm not sure

green: I really understand it

Summary

Three-part lessons accelerate learning. When planning careers lessons there should be both a starter activity and a plenary activity included in the plan to encourage colleagues to use them. This will increase the impact of learning in the classroom.

Chapter 12
WORK EXPERIENCE

- What is work experience?

- Models of work experience

- Progression in work experience

- Learning through work experience

- Making work experience effective

- Recording experiences of work

- Briefing and debriefing activities

- Relating work experience to the 14-19 work-related learning curriculum

- Summary

What is work experience?

Work experience is when a pupil goes to a place of work and carries out tasks related to a specific job under the direction of a supervisor. Work experience must take place on an employer's premises and so differs from school-based, work-related learning activities.

Some employers will not give the pupil the opportunity to carry out specific tasks related to a job. The pupil may be given things to keep them busy which are not job-specific, e.g. producing a poster to put in a shop window. Although the task may be valid, the placement should be termed 'experience of work' rather than 'work experience'. If no specific job-related tasks are carried out then the placement is work shadowing rather than work experience.

With true work experience the pupil will develop skills related to a specific job. They will be given responsibility to carry out tasks rather than just observing somebody else in their work role. Pupils will progress in the complexity of the work done during the placement.

Models of work experience

Block schemes

The block scheme involves a whole year group on placement at the same time. Work experience should be an entitlement for all pupils during KS4. As part of the social inclusion agenda pupils should not be withdrawn from the scheme except in extreme circumstances.

All pupils should experience a minimum of a week, and ideally two weeks, in the workplace. There are benefits and drawbacks associated with running the scheme for one week or for two. With one-week placements there is less time taken away from subject areas and more employers are willing to take pupils for only one week. The drawback is that one week gives less time for pupils to develop work-related skills and to gain a deep understanding of the workplace. There is also less time to build up positive working relationships which help to boost self-esteem. With a two-week placement the pupil often gets greater rewards and develops a sense of belonging. The disadvantage is that inevitably this will lead to a greater demand upon employers and the need for schools to find two placements for many pupils.

The post 16-curriculum should also allow pupils to undertake work experience for a minimum of a week. If pupils are seeking employment at 17 or 18 they should be given more time to develop work skills. Many HE courses require pupils to have had direct experience, e.g. for medicine, physiotherapy, veterinary science, media and law.

Vocational courses

Pupils may be following a vocational curriculum at GCSE and have a day a week on work placement related to their vocational area. For example, pupils undertaking a vocational GCSE in health and social care may spend a morning a week helping at a local play group. The total number of days may well exceed the ten days spent on block placement and it will certainly span a longer time period. This allows the pupil to develop greater understanding through the support of the taught curriculum and it also allows greater time for self-development. The nature of the tasks undertaken will also increase in complexity as the placement progresses.

Extended work training

This is for pupils who spend a proportion of their time during KS4 in the workplace. This may be for up to four days a week and allows pupils to be trained for a specific trade or job and, in some cases, to undertake NVQ assessments. This model is set to stay, with increased flexibility in the KS4 curriculum, the introduction of work-related learning for all in KS4, and the introduction of Individual Learning Plans for all pupils in year 9.

The aim is that pupils of all abilities who would benefit from work training should be offered this as an alternative to GCSEs. In practice at the moment work training is seen by many schools as a way of providing more appropriate education for disaffected young learners. However, this model should also be used to stretch gifted and talented pupils who could attain GCSEs early or in reduced curriculum time, allowing them time to enter the workplace with a high challenge placement.

Progression in work experience

There should be the opportunity for pupils to progress during a work placement but also to progress through placements undertaken in different years. During a placement pupils should be given the opportunity to develop skills. They should therefore be given new and more challenging tasks towards the end of a placement. If pupils face two weeks of filing or stocking shelves they will be less responsive to learning through their experience. Employers will vary in their awareness of this need and often placements will break down because of this lack of understanding. In these situations it is the work experience coordinator's role to go and negotiate what the pupil could do to give them some progression.

Progression should be planned for pupils who undertake work experience in more than one key stage. Typically a year 10 placement may be seen as providing the pupil with an experience of work without careful vocational targeting. The pupil would be assisted in finding a placement and be instructed on when and how to approach the employer. However, in a year 12 programme a pupil would first identify their own network, learn how to market themselves, learn how to target employers, learn how to make approaches appropriately by telephone, letter, email and face-to-face, with no set instruction on when and how to do this, leaving the responsibility and decision making with the pupil. Once they have secured a placement, the year 12 pupil would negotiate the programme with the employer, having thought through what they wish to achieve and what their personal targets are. A year 12 placement would be related to a pupil's specific needs and career ambition. Thus there is a clear progression from one key stage to the next.

Learning through work experience

Work experience provides a superb learning opportunity. Pupils are placed in situations which generate emotional responses, and this enhances the effect of the learning. If pupils spend time with a good supervisor the conversations relating to tasks helps to build a deep understanding. According to Vygotsky's social development theory it provides an excellent opportunity for collective learning in a social situation. With appropriate guidance before, during and after the placement the pupil can learn not only about work but more importantly about themselves. They can recognise and develop skills, qualities, attitudes, values and achievements which will be transferable to new situations.

To complete the stages of learning according to Gagne there must be effective preparation and debriefing for work experience. Without this the learning purpose will become lost to the pupil and they will not engage with the activity. It becomes obvious when a pupil has been poorly briefed for work experience and has not developed the understanding of why they are doing it. In this situation pupils will often sum up their experience as boring or good but they are unable to relate it to their own development.

Pupils who have been well prepared for their experience will be able to talk about what they have learned about themselves; how they have grown personally from the placement; what they have observed about other people; and what they have learned from that.

Making work experience effective

In order to choose an appropriate placement pupils should be aware of the following:

- what their level of attainment is likely to be

- what qualifications are needed for specific jobs

- that jobs can be grouped into job families which require similar skills and qualities

- what their dominant learning style is

- how learning styles can be related to job families

- what their skills and qualities are and how these relate to different jobs

- what types of employment are available locally

- labour market information

- what their values are relating to work

- what their goals are relating to work

- that choice should be free from stereotyping and discrimination.

This list highlights the need to have a good curriculum in place during KS3 which progresses during KS4. If pupils have developed this level of self-awareness and understanding about factors that impact on work choice then choosing placements is less of a lottery. Self-awareness also encourages pupils not just to take an easy option, which usually means going to work in a low-challenge situation with familiar people.

Developing communication skills is an important aim of work experience. All pupils should write a letter of introduction to their employer, make a formal telephone call, and go on a preplacement interview. Pupils approach the placement far more positively if they have visited the premises in advance and met their supervisor. A visit helps to reduce first-day nerves and helps mental preparation. Many pupils will find all these things challenging and daunting, and in some cases they will not have the confidence to carry the steps through. Skills development should be supported through the preparation programme. The tutor should monitor progress made and target support, helping less confident youngsters to make a telephone call and arrange an interview. If a pupil has specific learning needs it is a good idea for a member of the learning support team to contact the employer and negotiate an appropriate programme.

Pupils have poor experiences when the work they are doing does not suit their learning style, if it is repetitive and inappropriate to their ability, if there is no social forum within which they can learn and if they can see no value in the work. Good experiences happen when the opposite is true. In addition pupils should have individual goals for their experience so that they know what they are working towards and can recognise achievement and success. The goals should be recorded and communicated to the employer so that there is a shared understanding. In the simplest sense this could be the pupil recording in the log book three things they want to achieve during the placement. In a more complex sense it could form SMART targets with measured outcomes which are reported on by the employer. In both cases the pupil should monitor their progress during the placement and have review points to discuss it with their supervisor.

The progress made towards these goals should also be part of the discussion and review with the teacher who visits the placement. The placement works best when the visiting teacher has a relationship with the pupil, such as their tutor, head of year or subject teacher, which is particularly pertinent to vocational placements linked to courses. The teacher should be briefed on the type of conversation to have with the pupil. The visit is not merely to check if there are any problems but to lead discussions relating to self-development learning.

Recording experiences of work

Pupils should have a log book to take on work experience. It is a self-development manual, which records a pupil's self-learning, before, during and after the placement.

The pupil should be able to record the outcomes of their self-awareness preparation such as their preferred learning style, jobs which fit this profile, their minimum expectations, personal goals, etc. There should also be a format which allows them to record what they have learnt about letter writing, telephone skills and interview technique, with an integrated self-review.

During the placement the following could be recorded in the log book:

- their feelings towards the placement the evening before they go, their expectations and anxieties

- their first day feelings: how do they feel at the end of the first day?

- a review of their targets or goals, carried out at a few points through the placement

- a memory jogger in which to record specific work-related tasks

- a page to record specific health and safety instructions given during the placement

- a structured interview with an employee about their work and career route

- activities linked to a curriculum task which will vary according to the courses studied

- a reflection page to be completed towards the end of the placement: how have their feelings and attitudes changed during the placement?

- their achievements and successes

- the employer's report form and comment page.

These elements are the minimum required in the log book, and teachers should resist the temptation to produce a weighty booklet filled with activities and tasks. The pupils' main focus is to concentrate on the work placement, and for the log book less is more. If the amount of writing is too onerous pupils will be put off by it, and will be too physically and mentally tired to put much effort in. Try to encourage short concise responses. Use scales to colour in, smiley faces, circling words, etc.

The self-reflection after the placement should also be recorded in the log book.

Key points are:

- qualities recognised

- skills developed

- achievements

- goals met

- what they have learnt about themselves

The completed log book must have purpose for the young person. It is disheartening if nobody looks at it and there is no apparent follow-up. Ideally the tutor would review the log book and the achievements with the pupil. A minimum is to collect in the log book and write a comment about what has been recorded. The information collected should lead into debriefing activities. The finalised log book should be kept in the pupil's Progress File and be used to inform their summary document at the end of KS4.

Briefing and debriefing activities

Preparation

Preparation for work experience is done with the whole year group of pupils. This is delivered through the tutorial or PSHE time leading up to the placement. This is when self-awareness activities and decision making will be delivered, including work-related skills development such as letter writing and interview preparation. Health and safety activities should be included, such as spotting hazards and role playing how to deal with difficult situations.

Briefing

Briefing is separate from preparation because it operates on an individual level and is particular to a placement. As well as general health and safety awareness raising, pupils should be given advice and guidance specific to their job. One way to do this is to put pupils into job-type groupings with an employer from one of the placements to lead them through potential risks and hazards and behaviour expectations.

In addition, advice sent to participating employers makes it clear that they have a responsibility to give a health and safety briefing before the placement begins. This could be done during the preplacement interview or on the first day of the placement. Pupils must be made aware of this so that they can request a briefing, or can telephone the school to inform the work experience coordinator if they have not received one and have been sent out to begin work.

Debriefing

There should be some immediate debriefing followed by longer-term follow-up. Some schools involve the employers in this activity, which is desirable but not essential. There has to be a balance between the now flagging energy levels of the coordinator and tutors against the benefits to the pupils.

Immediate follow-up should include the following, but a wide variety of approaches can be used:

- collective celebration at bringing the year group back together

- structured oral discussion with one another about their experiences, e.g. circle time about what they have learnt

- sharing of achievements and successes

- producing a personal statement using the information collected in their log book

- formally thanking the employer.

Longer term feedback should include:

- recognising how the skills developed can be applied and used in new situations

- learning how to use evidence from work experience to market yourself for your next transition stage

- target-setting for goal achievement during year 11

- using the learning to inform decisions about options post-16.

The most important thing is not to belittle and ignore the enormous amount of self-learning that will have taken place during the experience.

Relating work experience to the 14-19 work-related learning curriculum

Work-related learning for all at KS4 is statutory from September 2004. The Framework sets out a minimum requirement for pupils to experience during this key stage. All pupils must learn through work, about work and for work. There are obvious implications for the work-experience programme to ensure that the learning that takes place is mapped against the Framework. Through the framework pupils must be given opportunities to do the following:

- *Recognise, develop and apply their skills for employability*: pupils recognise their skills and qualities and demonstrate how these will increase their employability. They should collect evidence of leadership, management, decision-making, innovative problem solving and self-reliance.

- *Use their experience of work, including work experience and part time work, to extend their understanding of work*: pupils should give an account of their work experience and apply their learning to career planning. Pupils analyse what motivates people for work and demonstrate an understanding of the main changes happening in the world of work.

- *Learn from contact with personnel from different employment sectors*: pupils should have direct contact with a minimum of two people from different work sectors. Many pupils will achieve this by undertaking two different placements. Others will learn from undertaking work experience that is different to part-time work. This has implications for guiding pupils for undertaking suitable placements which will allow the contrast to become apparent. Pupils will describe working practices in the two different sectors, understand career motivations and pathways, and understand also the importance to employers of attitudes, qualifications and skills.

- *Have experience of working environments and practices*: pupils will contrast the two different experiences of work by describing the work environment and the hazards associated with particular work placements.

These four points form nearly half of the statutory requirement for work-related learning. This means that the follow-up programme from work experience is crucial to maximise the learning potential. Pupils should be using part-time employment to compare and contrast the two different work environments and undertake follow-up activities at the start of year 11 to allow this to happen.

Summary

Work experience provides the most powerful opportunity for self-development. Our task is to make sure that the experience increases self-awareness and self-esteem and helps to prepare young learners for employability. A work experience placement should not be undertaken without a supporting learning programme in place.

Chapter 13
PROGRESS FILE

- What is a Progress File?

- What goes into a Progress File?

- The benefits of a Progress File

- Models of delivery

- Successful delivery

- Summary

What is a Progress File?

Schools have a statutory requirement from September 2004 to have in place a system that enables pupils to recognise and record their achievements, to monitor their progress, and to set targets in relation to these achievements and progress. This requirement is for the whole 11–19 age range with the hope that it will extend beyond this time frame and help to engender life-long learning habits.

Schools can either adopt their own system, or adopt the family of Progress Files published by the DfES, or combine the two. The term 'Progress File' may be used in two ways: it may relate to the version published by the DfES, or as a more general descriptor it may refer to school versions.

The document itself is not as important as the process and the impact that it has on young learners. It should not just be seen as a paper-based resource but as a working document that supports pupils' self-development with the individual at the heart of it. The ethos is that 'every child counts', that no individual in an institution should be overlooked and pass by unnoticed. It is based on a pupil-centred learning approach. It aims to encourage reflection and review, planning and recording, and it centres on both the academic and the pastoral care of a pupil. It supports learning, personal development and career planning.

What goes into a Progress File?

The type of contents in a Progress File may be:

- minimum expected grade data
- academic targets and their review
- personal development targets
- action points from reports
- short- and long-term goals
- barriers to achieving goals
- aspirations
- achievements
- rewards
- responsibility cards or awards
- personal skills and qualities, and evidence to support this
- reflection on participation
- recording of learning points from personal development activities
- evidence of being an active citizen in the school community and in the local community
- self-evaluation of participation in tutorial activities
- careers guidance action plans
- career planning
- Individual Learning Plans and their yearly reviews
- information on learning styles
- learning outcomes from work experience, employer reports, personal accounts, etc.

The list is long but the overall aim is holistic. The individual is at the centre of the learning process and a Progress File provides a central point for the pupil to see themselves as one person navigating their way through school with individual needs, rather than a part of a cohort.

A Progress File is essentially a ring binder to which material is added, and from which some is pruned, as the pupil moves through the weeks, terms and years. Activities undertaken should be pertinent to the child's needs at that time. A programme is needed to support the use of the folder, which is time-based and directly relevant to pupils' experiences. For example, there should be a section in year 10 that is relevant to going to a work experience interview, with inbuilt self-review. If there is a whole-school production at Christmas, there should be a mechanism for recording their achievement through the Progress File, etc.

If a school devises its own system it is more likely to relate directly to the pupils of that school and support their development in a synchronised way. The home-grown version should give more sense of ownership. If pupils and tutors are involved in the review and evaluation process it will become a powerful tool with a school and year-group identity. A bespoke Progress File allows for flexibility and can respond to needs immediately through its adaptability. Pupils can record achievements in a number of ways and may choose to include photographs and personal accounts of events, witness statements and feedback. They may wish to include certificates, letters of commendation, and pieces of work of which they are proud. Ideally each Progress File should end up being as individual as the person themself, with the pupil selecting what is important to them.

If the DfES Progress File family is adopted, a school should look to personalise it and use it with discrimination. It is a good starting point for a school that has nothing in place.

There are four publications for the key stages:

Getting started (KS3)

Moving on (KS4)

Widening horizons (post-16)

Broadening horizons (adult and HE).

The benefits of a Progress File

A Progress File provides a powerful mechanism for pupils to organise information about themselves, to increase their self-awareness and enhance progress in all aspects of their life, in and out of school. The benefits are as follows.

- Pupils are put at the centre of their own learning.

- Achievements are recognised, which helps to increase self-esteem.

- Pupil motivation is increased with the desire to succeed.

- Targets are regularly reviewed and monitored so that the pupil can recognise that progress is being made, leading to greater achievement.

- Pupils with clear career plans find greater meaning in what school is about for them, and it helps to sharpen the learning focus.

- Good habits are developed of recognising positive aspects of themselves and their lives which helps to build self-esteem.

- Evidence collection is encouraged, which helps pupils to build up their own personal portfolio which can support them at transition times.

- Pupils are more able to present themselves positively and confidently to others on paper and face-to-face because they recognise their strengths and transferable skills.

- Pupils are better prepared for transition stages because each has been planned and is a part of a life plan rather than a discrete event.

- It provides a good document for tracking the individual pupil so that one-to-one interviews have a sharper focus.

The underlying key message is that schools are not only about putting pupils through qualifications but about developing individuals who will be active citizens fitting into society with positive home and work relationships. Having pieces of paper in a folder will not achieve this. However, talking to people about themselves and their self-learning will have more of an impact.

Models of delivery

Progress Files are an excellent resource if used frequently and habitually by pupils. To allow this to happen their must be a structure in which use of a Progress File is embedded. There are several models of delivery:

- through a tutorial period overseen by the tutor

- combined into a self-development curriculum of PSHE, RE and citizenship, overseen by a specialist teacher

- used to underpin discrete PSHE lessons overseen by specialist teachers

- through frequent collapsed timetable periods, e.g. four times per term.

For true ownership by pupils they must have access to the Progress File when they need it, e.g. to add in certificates. For this reason the most successful model appears to be one where the folders are stored in the tutorial base and they are used by pupils at least once a week in tutorial time.

Successful delivery

Research into the use of Progress Files has been carried out through piloting the project and through case studies. Some key messages arise from this research about how to ensure success.

- Right timing should be ensured by using Progress Files as part of the target-setting review.

- Senior management teams must have a high profile in the introduction and implementation of Progress Files.

- Progress Files must complement and underpin existing activities instead of being a bolt-on.

- Tutors must be committed, and publicly recognise the worth of Progress Files with pupils.

- There must be allocated time for activities.

- Pupils must have ownership.

- Pupils must have easy access to their folders.

- Role models who have made successful transitions can be invited to assemblies.

- Staff should model the use of Progress Files by using the same approach for their own CPD.

- Implementation of Progress Files must link to other initiatives, e.g. the Healthy Schools award.

- Mentors should be trained in the use of Progress Files and use them as a format for their meetings with pupils.

The way in which the idea of Progress Files is introduced to staff and pupils is crucial. They must be seen as part of a long-term commitment to putting pupils at the centre of their own learning. The files and activities are pointless unless the deliverer comes across as being enthusiastic and committed. There must be a system in place for monitoring their use at the point of impact, and heads of year should have a role in work sampling to ensure consistency within their year group. There should be ongoing evaluation, ensuring that each year the file is slightly different in response to the changes happening across a school.

Summary

There is a statutory requirement on a school to have a progress monitoring system in place. There are many benefits to using a progress filing system as long as the implementation is effective and all partners recognise its worth and importance.